CALENDAR COMPANIONS

For Winter

written by

Susanne Glover
and
Georgeann Grewe

illustrated by Georgeann Grewe

Cover by Gary Mohrmann
Copyright © Good Apple, Inc., 1984
ISBN No. 0-86653-168-8

Good Apple, Inc.
A Division of Frank Schaffer Publications, Inc.
23740 Hawthorne Boulevard,
Torrance, CA 90505-5927

The purchase of this book entitles the buyer to reproduce student activity pages for classroom use only. Any other use requires written permission from Good Apple, Inc.

This book is dedicated to:
Thelma L. Grewe
George E. Grewe
Amy E. Glover
Russell H. Glover

TABLE OF CONTENTS

DECEMBER:

Cover Sheet iv
Teacher Tips 1
Calendar 3
Bulletin Boards 5
Penmanship 12
Language Arts 13
Math 19
Science 22
Social Studies 24
Art 31
Music 33
Citizenship 34
Patterns 36
Answer Key 40

JANUARY:

Cover Sheet 41
Teacher Tips 42
Calendar 44
Bulletin Boards 46
Penmanship 53
Language Arts 54
Math 62
Science 66
Social Studies 68
Art 69
Music 72
Citizenship 73
Nutrition 74
Patterns 75
Answer Key 81

FEBRUARY:

Cover Sheet 82
Teacher Tips 83
Calendar 85
Bulletin Boards 87
Penmanship 94
Language Arts 95
Math 105
Science 108
Social Studies 112
Art 113
Music 116
Citizenship 118
Patterns 119
Answer Key 124

Teacher Tips

DECEMBER (page iv)
* Use as a coloring sheet.
* Use as a cover for a December booklet of work sheets or projects.

CALENDAR (page 3)
* Add numbers for dates, **Calendar Creations** information (page 4), and/or pictures in appropriate boxes.
* List birthdays of classmates.
* Use as a monthly weather guide.
* Assign research for gifted children to create their own calendar events.

CALENDAR CREATIONS (page 4)
* Allow students to research topics and report findings to class.
* Announce events in opening exercises each day.

STOCKING STUFFERS FOR SANTA (pages 5-8)
* Make this bulletin board to display good papers after students complete the creative writing assignments on the backs of toys in and around the stocking.
* Use the bulletin board to display spelling, reading, vocabulary, or **Word Wizard** words which could be written on objects in the stocking.
* Change bulletin board title to "How Does Your Stocking Add Up?" and write numbers on the toys in the stocking for children to add.

PUR-R-FECT PENMANSHIP (page 12)
* Read and discuss the poem orally with the class, discussing format, rhyme, capital letters and punctuation before assigning children to copy the poem in their best writing.

WORD WIZARD (page 13)
* Use the words as a spelling list for the month.
* Assign topics for research projects.
* Use the list as an answer sheet for several words found on the work sheet **Wordsworth** on page 14.

CHRISTMAS COUPLETS (page 15)
* Review the poetic form for couplets; read and discuss the couplets presented; assist children in writing their own couplets.

LETTER OUTLINE (page 18)
* Give children this form to write home about their progress.

> Dear Mom and Dad,
>   Here is my work for the month
> of December. Please look at it so
> you will see how I am progressing . . . .

SUM SURPRISES (pages 19-20)
* Provide each student with copies of these work sheets to complete.
* Use the same ideas found on the work sheet, but let children add their own words made from the letters on the packages.
* Ask children to find the most expensive and the least expensive combinations of packages found on the work sheet on page 20.

CHRISTMAS PLANTS (pages 22-23)
* Distribute copies of this sheet and **The Christmas Tree Story** to use as background information for science (evergreens).
* Ask children to illustrate and color various evergreens to display in the classroom.
* Use information written on the bulbs on pages 25-29 to introduce the social studies/language arts legends for Christmas.

CHRISTMAS TREE AND TRIM (pages 24-29)
* Use this story for language arts or social studies to familiarize children with various legends about the Christmas tree; provide each child with a copy of the material, the cover sheet (bulb) and five pages of background, to be cut out, stapled, and colored to make a booklet.

CHRISTMAS TREES SOLD BY WHITEY PINE (page 30)
* Review picture graphs and keys with the class before giving out copies of this work sheet to be completed.

A FINE PINE TO MAKE (pages 31-32)
* Follow the directions given to complete this three-dimensional Christmas tree; display finished trees in the room.
* Use the same idea for the tree and branches but use in conjunction with the **Giving Tree** theme for an Advent project (see pages 34-35).

MINI UNIT -- THE CHRISTMAS TREE
* This could be prepared as an all-day unit for intermediate or primary children. Choose work sheets in this packet to include all content areas. Our suggestions include:
  1. **December** cover sheet for booklet about the Christmas tree (page iv).
  2. **Pur-r-fect Penmanship** work sheet for writing (page 12).
  3. **Word Wizard** and **Wordsworth** work sheet for language arts (pages 13-14).
  4. **Spruce Up Your Math** story problem work sheet (page 21).
  5. **The Christmas Tree Story** for science, to be used perhaps as an introduction for **The Christmas Tree and Trim** booklet which follows for social studies (pages 23-29).
  6. **Christmas Tree** graph for social studies (page 30).
  7. **A Fine Pine** lesson and work sheet for art (pages 31-32).

Slight preparations may be necessary as the activities are adapted to the needs of your classroom. You may wish to supplement with some of your own materials.

Calendar Creations

DECEMBER:

2	EPA (Environmental Protection Agency) established
3	Public preview of jumbo jet 747
5	Walt Disney's birthday
7	Japan attacked Pearl Harbor
8	Bird Banding Association established
9	John Milton's birthday
10	Human Rights' Day
	Emily Dickinson's birthday
16	Ludwig van Beethoven's birthday
	Margaret Mead's birthday
17	Flight of Wright brothers' airplane at Kitty Hawk
18	Ty Cobb's birthday
19	First cotton mill established by Samuel Slater
21	Newspaper (NEW YORK WORLD) published first crossword puzzle
22	First day of winter
	Lincoln Tunnel opened between New York and New Jersey
23	Astronauts orbited moon for first time (Apollo VIII)
24	Kit Carson's birthday
25	Christmas Day
27	Radio City Music Hall opened
	Louis Pasteur's birthday
28	Chewing gum patented
	Woodrow Wilson's birthday
30	Rudyard Kipling's birthday
31	New Year's Eve

STOCKING STUFFERS FOR SANTA

YOU WILL NEED:

1. Yellow background
2. Bright green letters for title
3. Large red stocking (could use real stocking for 3-D effect)
4. Several toys made from patterns on the following two pages, colored, labeled, and laminated to display in and around stocking
5. A few copies of the story page to display on board

DIRECTIONS:

On the back of each toy displayed on the bulletin board, write a topic for creative writing. Let children choose a toy and complete the writing assignment on a sheet of paper or use the penmanship page provided (page 8). Display work.

PATTERNS

Make several copies of these patterns on oaktag. Color them. On the back of the object, write a creative writing topic. Laminate these and display them on the bulletin board around the stocking. Use this bulletin board as a station for individuals or as a total class project.

PATTERNS

_____

_____

_____

_____

_____

_____

_____

_____

_____

_____

_____

_____

_____

_____

_____ NAME

TREE BORDER

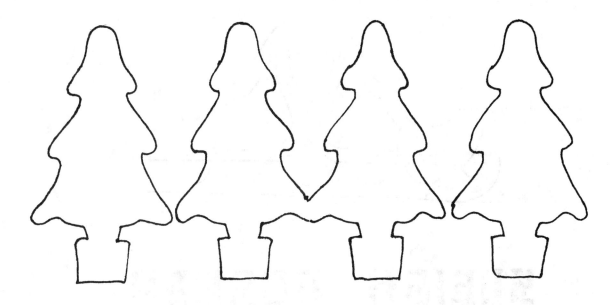

Measure the bulletin board surface you wish to cover. Cut as many strips as you will need. Fold strips in half and then in half again.

Trace the tree or make a copy as shown. Place the pattern on your folded strip of paper. Trace around it. Cut it out except where the object lies on the fold. You will have four trees when you unfold the paper. You may want to use the border at the top and bottom only to make your bulletin board attractive!

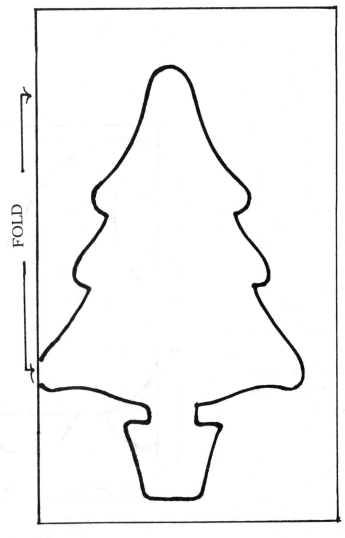

FOLD

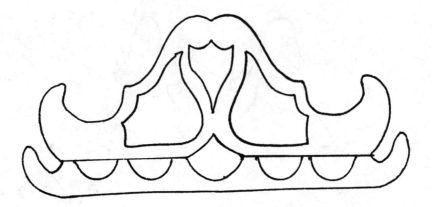

SLEIGH BORDER

This sleigh will add a fancy touch to that December bulletin board.

Directions may be found on page 9.

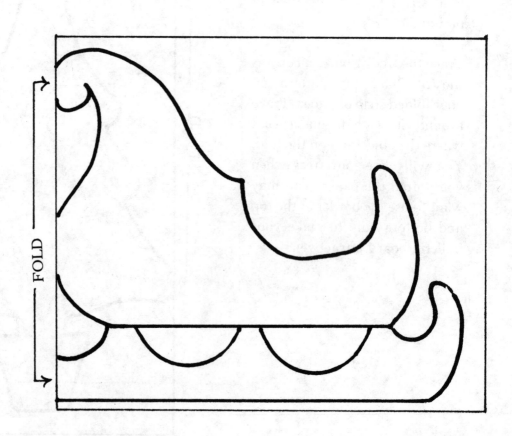

FOLD

CANDY CANE BORDER

This bold border is certain to attract attention to your bulletin board.

For directions, refer to page 9.

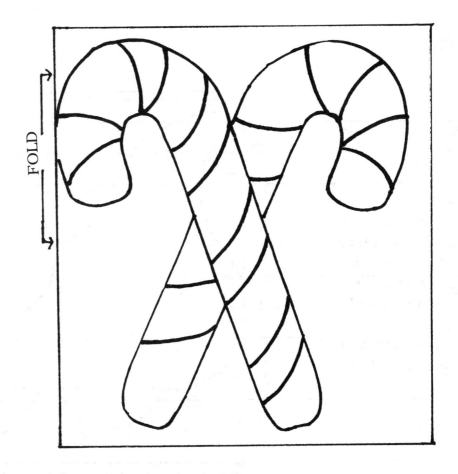

Pur-r-fect Penmanship

THE PINE

A tree stands in the woods by our house
It's a pine, an evergreen--
From our window we can see it,
Laden with snow, what a scene!

Its branches seem to bow and arch
In just the perfect way.
Cones among the needles hide
As if a game they play!

We'll cut it down and carry it
Into the house, you see.
Add star, bulbs, lights and tinsel,
To make our Christmas tree.

WORD WIZARD

1. poinsettia
2. Advent
3. New Year's Eve
4. cookies
5. Christmas
6. ribbon
7. card
8. crèche
9. stocking
10. shopping
11. St. Nicholas
12. angel
13. sleigh
14. manger
15. candle
16. holly
17. Santa Claus
18. wreath
19. star
20. winter
21. party
22. Hanukkah
23. tinsel
24. wrapping
25. bell
26. carol
27. decoration
28. present
29. tree
30. candy cane

WORDSWORTH

On a sheet of paper, write down any words that you find in the maze. You may double any letter or repeat used letters as you spell words. Each letter in your word will be worth one point. If a word is on your Word Wizard list, double points for that word.

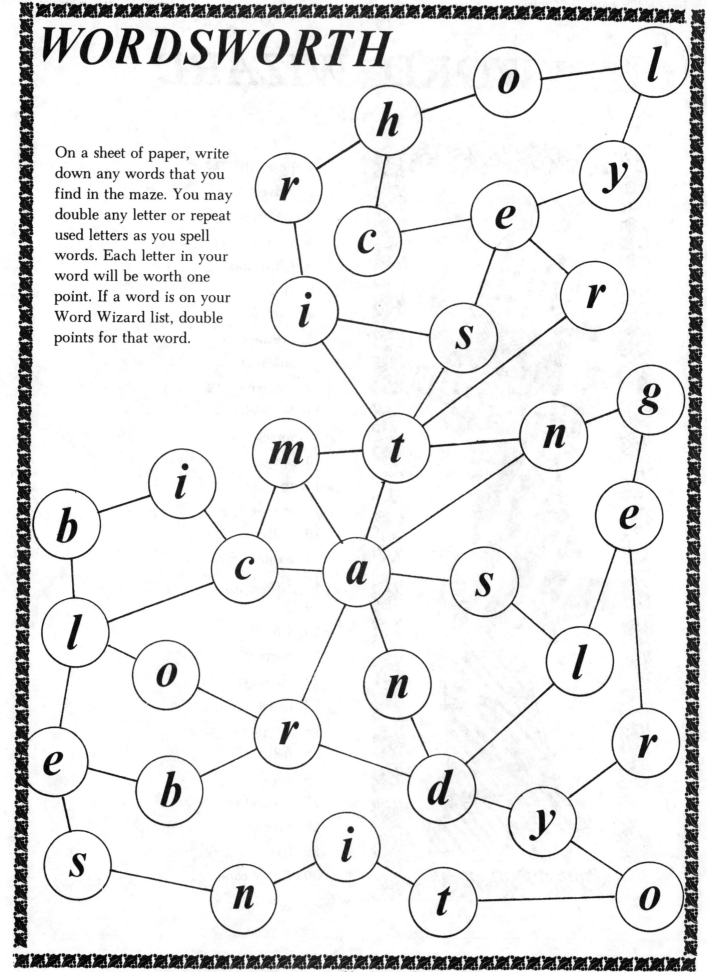

CHRISTMAS COUPLETS

Here is one of the easiest types of poetry. It is a COUPLET. Each couplet is a two-line thought that rhymes. Read the couplets below and then try to write some of your own.

In the winter when it snows,
I catch a cold and blow my nose.

Snowflakes falling to the earth
Showing off our winter's birth.

Presents wrapped under the tree,
Some for you and some for me.

Stockings hanging in a row
Filled with treats from top to toe.

Baking cookies, making sweets,
To give to friends for holiday treats.

Candles with their flames aglow
Spreading warmth and cheer below.

Out on the lawn stands the evergreen --
Boughs laden with snow — a beautiful scene.

Now you try.

1. _____

_____

2. _____

_____

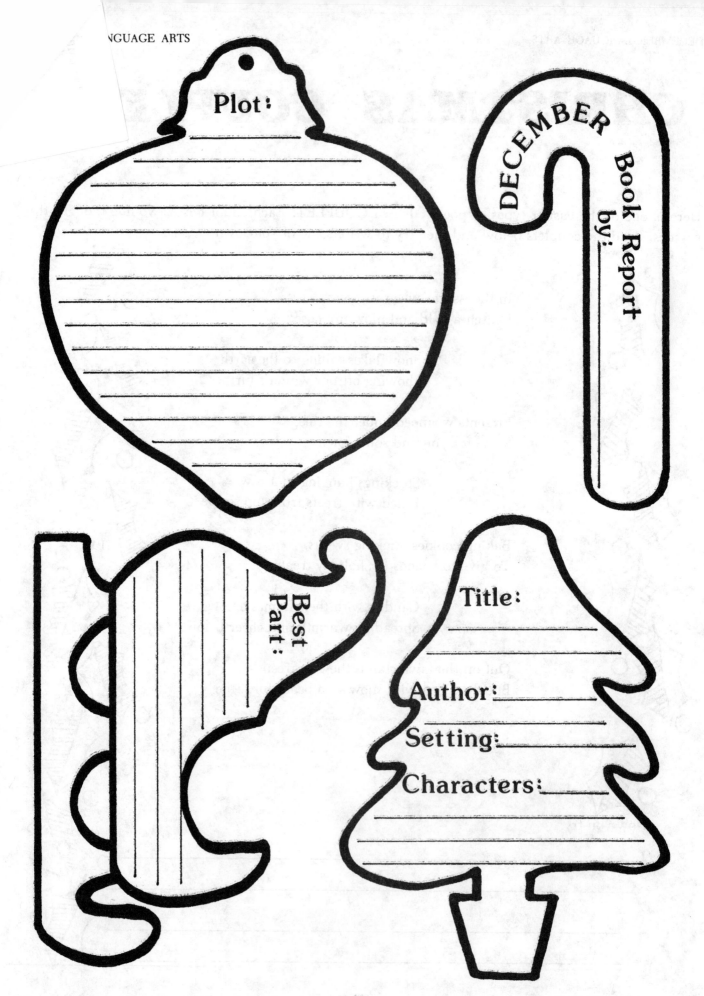

Plot:

DECEMBER Book Report by:

Best Part:

Title:

Author:

Setting:

Characters:

SUM SURPRISES

(Use the work sheet on the next page with this one.)

Sum Surprises Work Sheet

_____   NAME   _____   DATE

FIND THE VALUE OF THESE PACKAGES:

①   H _____
   + E _____

②.   C _____
   + A _____
     B _____

③.   D _____
   + I _____
     G _____

④.   I _____
   + F _____

⑤.   H _____
     I _____
   + D _____
     E _____

⑥.   B _____
     A _____
   + D _____
     G _____
     E _____

⑦.   B _____
     E _____
   + A _____
     D _____

⑧.   A _____
   + C _____
     E _____

Good bulletin board

SPRUCE UP YOUR MATH

Dad bought 24 white pine, 38 spruce, 17 cedar, and 56 Douglas fir trees. How many trees did Dad buy in all?

1.

Last year my family planted 1,057 evergreens. If we sold 692 of them, how many are left?

2.

Uncle Joe has a tree farm. If he planted 35 rows of holly bushes and there are 14 bushes in a row, how many bushes does he have?

3.

My brother and I collected 945 pinecones. We carried 35 in each basket. How many baskets did it take?

4.

For Christmas, Mom bought 4 wreaths that cost $14.95 each. She also got 5 stockings for $3.75 each. How much did Mom spend in all?

5.

Nancy bought a box of tree lights for $4.95 and 3 boxes of ornaments for $4.50 each. What change would she get from $50.00?

6.

Mom gave my three sisters and me a fifty dollar bill. How much money would we each get if we split the money equally?

7.

21

CHRISTMAS PLANTS

HOLLY was once considered sacred by the pagans. In modern times it has become a symbol of peace and joy. In olden days it was said that people often settled quarrels beneath the holly tree.

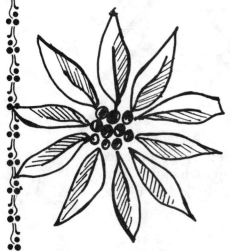

The **POINSETTIA** was brought to the United States by Dr. Joel Poinsett. A legend from Mexico tells about a poor girl with no gift to offer the Virgin Mary, so she picked some flowering weeds. As soon as she placed them before Mary's statue, beautiful poinsettia flowers blossomed.

Ancient Greeks believed that the **MISTLETOE** would keep away evil. They believed it would cure sicknesses and bring about a happy marriage. People of today sometimes think that if mistletoe falls to the ground that it is unlucky. Another belief is that a girl standing under it cannot refuse to be kissed. If she goes unkissed then she cannot expect to be married the next year.

ROSEMARY, an evergreen now used to season foods, was once a popular Christmas plant. In the Middle Ages women spread it on the floor at Christmas. As people walked on it, a fragrant smell filled the room. Legend tells that the plant has a fragrant aroma because Mary laid the clothes of Christ on its branches.

THE CHRISTMAS TREE STORY

1. New pine trees come from pinecones. The cones are made of scales that fold over each other. Under the scales are tiny seeds.

IT TAKES
5-6 YEARS FOR
TREES TO GROW
LARGE ENOUGH
TO BE USED
FOR CHRISTMAS.

2. The seeds will not come out of the cones until the cones are brown and dry.

3.

The seeds are very small --- about the size of a period in a sentence. It takes only **one** tiny seed to grow up into a tall, beautiful tree.

MAKE YOUR OWN
CHRISTMAS TREE!
TAKE THE SEEDS
FROM A DRY PINE CONE.
PUT THEM ON A
MOIST BLOTTER TO
SPROUT. WAIT 5 YRS

PINE NEEDLES
MAKE FOOD
FOR THE PINE TREE.

4. All seeds have a seed cover or seed coat. When they are put into soil, they will grow.

IN HAWAII PEOPLE
DECORATE LIVE
PALM TREES
FOR
CHRISTMAS
TREES.

5. When rain falls on the ground, it gets to the seed. Rain makes the seed coat soft. The inside of the seed begins to get larger. When this happens, the seed coat splits open.

PINE TREES ARE USED
TO MAKE PAPER. PER-
HAPS YOUR CHRISTMAS
WRAP CAME FROM
A PINE TREE.

6. The part of the seed that pushes down into the ground is the ROOT. The other part that pushes upward into the sunlight is the TRUNK with leaves and branches.

The Christmas Tree and Trim

Although trees hold a special place in the celebration of the Christian holiday of Christmas, the origin of this custom is uncertain. During the times of the Roman Empire, buildings were decorated with evergreens for the Festival of Saturnalia. Saturn was a god the Romans worshipped — a god of plenty. The evergreens, the plants that would not die because they were forever green, were thought to bring good luck. They were thought to hold magic and the hope that the sun would return during the cold, dark winter season. These trees and branches decorated windows and doors.

One legend states that three trees stood beside the stable where Jesus was born. To give glory to Him, the olive tree gave olives, the palm tree gave dates, and the pine tree had nothing of value to give Jesus. The stars shining above realized this. Some of them came down and rested on its branches as a gift to Jesus.

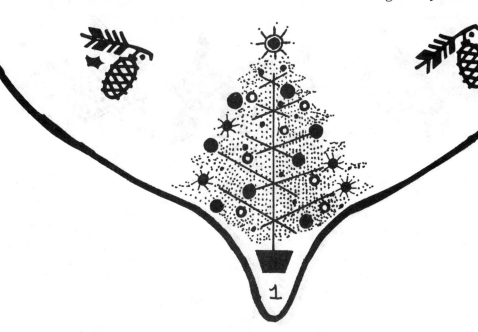

1

Another story is told about the Christmas tree in which a miracle happened. A missionary named Winfred was in Germany trying to convert the pagans. Just as they were about to sacrifice a little Prince, Winfred stopped them. He cut down the oak tree, and immediately a fir tree sprang up in its place. Winfred said the tree was the symbol of Christ and should be taken into their homes. Later, Winfred became known as St. Boniface.

In the 1600's there was a man named Martin Luther living in Germany. He was walking in the woods one evening, and he noticed the stars and white snow reflecting a beautiful light on the pines. To capture some of this beauty, it is said that he cut down a fir tree. When he got home, he added a few candles to the branches to create the scene for his children to enjoy.

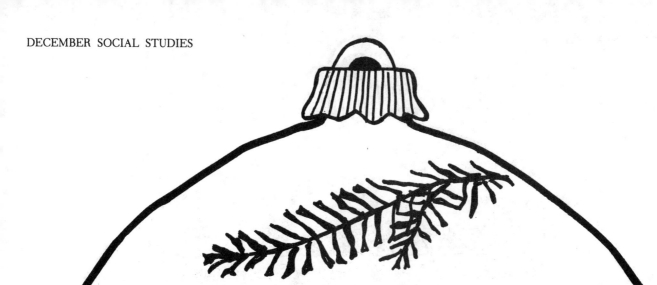

During the Revolutionary War it is said that the Hessians brought the Christmas tree custom to the United States. By the late 1800's, Sunday schools popularized the Christmas tree. The desire to bring the tree into individual homes was spreading, with spruce, fir, and pine being the favorites.

Just as Christmas trees were becoming popular in homes around the world, so, too, were the decorations for them. At first, homemade objects were used. Berries, popcorn, feathers, cookies, and fruits were hung on the branches. Straw ornaments were used as a symbol of grain — a symbol of food and good fortune. Later, bits of colored paper and finally glass bulbs were added. Horns and bells were sometimes used to ward off evil spirits.

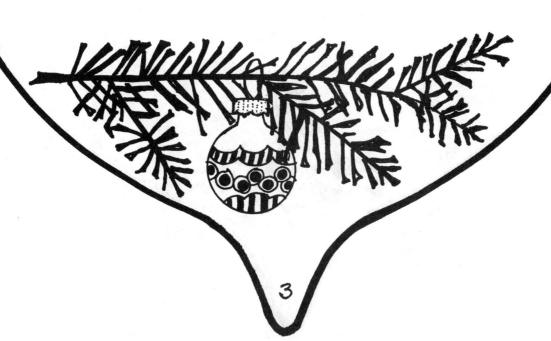

3

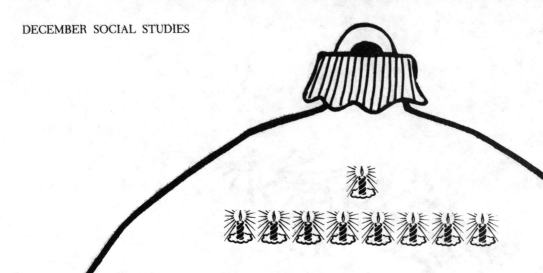

In the days of Martin Luther, candles lighted the Christmas tree, but not without caution. A wet sponge or water was kept near the tree in case of fire. Candles were thought to shed the special blessings of joy, light, and warmth. With the discovery of electricity, lights replaced the lighted candles. Today, electric candles, bells, drums, balls, and various other shapes are used to light the Christmas tree.

No tree would be complete without a special ornament on top. Although angels are sometimes used, the star is more popular. Stars have always seemed to hold some magical power. Sailors used stars to give direction, as did the Wise Men as they

4

28

travelled to Bethlehem. Some Indians believed the stars were once human beings, and they worshipped them. Three stars in a row were a symbol for a god. Today, an asterisk is a sign of something important. Stars have been signs throughout the centuries of hopes and dreams, so perhaps the star on top of your tree will bring you good luck and happiness during this Christmas season.

5

Christmas Trees sold by Whitey Pine

MONDAY 🌲🌲🌲🌲🌲

TUESDAY 🌲🌲🌲

WEDNESDAY 🌲🌲🌲🌲🌲🌲

THURSDAY 🌲🌲🌲🌲🌲

FRIDAY 🌲🌲🌲🌲🌲🌲🌲🌲🌲

SATURDAY 🌲🌲🌲🌲🌲🌲🌲🌲🌲🌲🌲🌲

Key: 🌲 = 10 Trees

Write True or False in the blanks.

1. The title of the graph tells the price of the trees. _____

2. On Wednesday 60 trees were sold. _____

3. More trees were sold at the end of the week than at the beginning. _____

4. The same number of trees was sold on Tuesday and Thursday. _____

5. Ten more trees were sold on Wednesday than Monday. _____

6. The most trees were sold on Friday. _____

7. On Friday, 20 less trees were sold than on Saturday. _____

8. The fewest number of trees was sold on Thursday. _____

9. On Friday and Saturday, 220 trees were sold._____

A Fine Pine to Make

Each child will need one tree and two pages of the star and branches from the following page. Use green construction paper. (Each child will have an extra star.)

25
20 11 6
1 14
17
10 2
7 21
24 19
15 3 12
4 23
22 9
13 16
18 5 8

Each child will cut out branches and glue them to the tree, forming layers.

Each child will use the star pattern and make a yellow star to glue to the top!

31

Star and Branches for Tree

Take NOTE for December!

Here are some suggestions for bringing music to your classroom this month:

1. Tape-record several popular Christmas carols. Play "Name that Tune" by skipping around to various parts of the tape and asking students to record some titles on their papers. (Records may also be used.)

2. Ask children to list on paper as many animals as they can recall which are mentioned in Christmas carols. Examples: deer - "Rudolph," cattle - "Away in a Manger."

3. Let children dramatize a Christmas carol and have other students guess the song title.

4. Choreograph a dance to a Christmas record and teach it to the class. "Jingle Bells" is an easy one!

5. Divide the class into several teams, each team selecting a secretary. Allow teams about 10 minutes to record as many Christmas carols as they can. After a designated time, let each group sing at least 4 lines of one of their carols to the class. All teams must eliminate carols which are sung. The winning team will be the one who sings the most songs without repeating any. A team which repeats is out!

6. Play a Christmas record and let students illustrate it (or one of their own choosing). Display finished work.

7. Assign each group of students a Christmas carol and let them make puppets to act out the song.

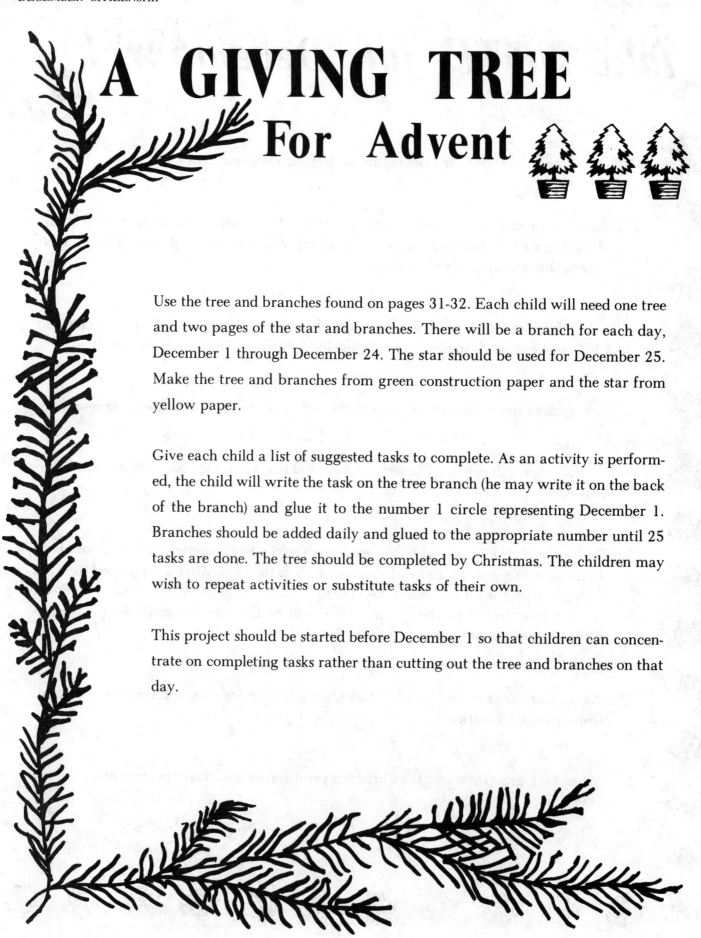

A GIVING TREE
For Advent

Use the tree and branches found on pages 31-32. Each child will need one tree and two pages of the star and branches. There will be a branch for each day, December 1 through December 24. The star should be used for December 25. Make the tree and branches from green construction paper and the star from yellow paper.

Give each child a list of suggested tasks to complete. As an activity is performed, the child will write the task on the tree branch (he may write it on the back of the branch) and glue it to the number 1 circle representing December 1. Branches should be added daily and glued to the appropriate number until 25 tasks are done. The tree should be completed by Christmas. The children may wish to repeat activities or substitute tasks of their own.

This project should be started before December 1 so that children can concentrate on completing tasks rather than cutting out the tree and branches on that day.

Suggested Giving Tree Tasks

1. Help a friend build a snowman.

2. Shovel or sweep the sidewalks.

3. Carry wood for the fireplace.

4. Gather pinecones for some Christmas decorations.

5. Learn a Christmas song and sing it to the class.

6. Make breakfast for your mom or dad.

7. Draw pictures of three Christmas plants to display at school.

8. Wash the dishes for your mom.

9. Write a letter to a friend or a relative.

10. Find a Christmas legend to present to your class.

11. Get the mail for your neighbor today.

12. Read a Christmas story to someone.

13. Wish your teacher a Happy Day and do something special for her.

14. Get some kind of exercise today to keep your body in good physical shape.

15. Bake some cookies or a treat for someone.

16. Make a decoration for the Christmas tree.

17. Do an extra chore for Mom or Dad today.

18. Take your pet for a walk or play with him.

19. Make a Christmas card and give it to someone special.

20. Show your parents three of your best papers for this month.

21. Do a chore for your brother or sister today.

22. Take the newspaper to Dad or Mom to read.

23. Make a special gift for someone.

24. Do some extra credit work for your teacher.

25. Memorize a Christmas poem (at least 8 lines) and recite it to your class.

Suggestions:

1. Add lines to this paper to make a Letter to Santa work sheet.
2. Have children cut out pictures of toys from catalogs to glue on bag. Ask them to write prices beside objects. Find most expensive toy, least expensive, etc.

Suggestions:
1. Have children research various Christmas customs and write their findings on trees to display in the room.
2. Have children write their own Christmas traditions practiced in their homes on the trees to be shared in class.

Suggestions:

1. Write creative writing topics on different boxes to place under a large tree on a bulletin board or at a writing center.
2. On the back of each package, write the name of an item. On the front, write adjectives to describe item for children to guess.

Suggestions:
1. Use the candle on the cover of a Christmas card. Either color it or make it from colored construction paper.
2. Write different prepositional or adverbial phrases on the holly leaves. Ask children to compose sentences using the phrases and write them on the candles.

ANSWER KEY

PAGE 14
Answers from Word Wizard
List might include:

1. star
2. angel
3. candy
4. holly
5. manger
6. candle

7. carol
8. Christmas
9. Santa
10. card
11. bell
12. tinsel

PAGE 30
1. false
2. true
3. true
4. false
5. true
6. false
7. false
8. false
9. true

PAGE 20
1. $ 10.45
2. $ 49.39
3. $125.28
4. $114.79

5. $121.14
6. $ 81.48
7. $ 66.89
8. $ 33.90

PAGE 21
1. 135 trees
2. 365 left
3. 490 bushes
4. 27 baskets
5. $78.55 spent
6. $31.55 change
7. $12.50 each

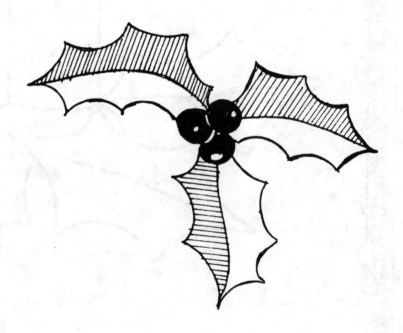

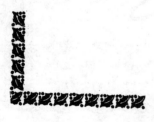

JANUARY

Happy New Year

Teacher Tips

JANUARY (page 41)

* Use as a coloring sheet.
* Use as a cover for a January booklet of work sheets or projects.

CALENDAR (page 44)

* Add numbers for dates, **Calendar Creations** information (page 45), and/or pictures in appropriate boxes.
* List birthdays of classmates.
* Use as a monthly weather guide.
* Assign research for gifted children to create their own calendar events.

CALENDAR CREATIONS (page 45)

* Allow students to research topics and report findings to class.
* Announce events in opening exercises each day.

SNEAK PREVIEW (pages 46-47)

* Make this bulletin board to display New Year's resolutions for the class after they complete the art lesson provided.
* Use the same title but use as an introductory bulletin board for September, substituting goals for the school year instead of New Year's resolutions.

SNOWFLAKE SHOWPLACE (pages 48-50)

* Display on this bulletin board a large completed snowflake person for the children to view; provide all materials in packets on the bulletin board so that this art station is complete.
* Change bulletin board title to "Students' Showplace" and use it to display good work.

PUR-R-FECT PENMANSHIP (page 53)

* Read and discuss the poem orally with your class, discuss format, rhyme, capital letters, and punctuation before assigning children to copy the poem.

WORD WIZARD (page 54)

* Use the words as a spelling list for the month.
* Assign topics for research projects.

WORD FACTORY (page 55)

* Duplicate this page and allow the class time to complete it.
* Ask students to create their own **Word Factories,** using words from their weekly spelling lists.

BUILD A SNOWMAN (pages 56-58)

* Provide the dice, snowmen, and game pieces so that children can play the game.
* Provide patterns and paper so that the class can make their own game.
* Change the title to "Build an Eskimo" and vary dice and game pieces accordingly.

THREE CHEERS (page 59)

* Use school cheers to introduce this lesson (use cheerleaders to demonstrate, if possible) and review purposes of cheers; then review the cheers written for the new year; assist students with composing their own cheers, perhaps with motions.
* Ask students who composed cheers to perform them for the class.

LETTER OUTLINE (page 61)
* Give children this form to write home about their progress.

  Dear Mom and Dad,

  Here is my work for the month of January.

  Please look at it so you will see how I

  am progressing . . . .

SNOWBALL BATTLE (pages 62-63)
* Write story problems on game cards, duplicate gameboard and cards for class.
* Use game cards to reinforce spelling words, reading vocabulary, or math or social studies facts.

A SNOWMAN'S SOLUTION (page 64)
* Use the same picture but make problems easier or more difficult to suit grade level.

SUB-ZERO SUBTRACTION (page 65)
* Insert problems of your choice but use the same work sheet design.

SNOW BUSINESS (page 66-67)
* Distribute a copy of this information and review it so that the class can proceed with the science activities on the following page.
* Do the activities with the class or assign them to be completed independently.

IF IT SNOWS...I (page 68)
* Review bar graphs with the class before distributing the work sheet to be completed.

FLIP OVER THIS (page 70)
* Follow directions on this page for making a "flip book"; do this activity with the class or set it up as a station.
* Introduce the flip book using the melting snowman concept; then let children choose their own concepts to illustrate.

START THE NEW YEAR (page 72)
* Teach the songs provided to the class (try them in rounds).
* Let children choose their own simple tunes and write their own verses to sing with them.

MINI UNIT--SNOW

This could be prepared as an all-day unit for intermediate or primary children. Choose work sheets in this packet to include all content areas. Our suggestions include:

1. **January** cover sheet for booklet about snow (page 41)
2. **Snowflake Showplace** bulletin board and art project (pages 48-50)
3. **Word Wizard** and **Word Factory** for language arts (pages 54-55)
4. **Build a Snowman** game to play, if time permits (pages 56-58)
5. **A Snowman's Solution** for math (page 64)
6. **Snow Business** to use with science activities (pages 66-67)
7. **If It Snows** bar graph for social studies (page 68)
8. **Start the New Year on a Happy Note** for music (page 72)
9. **Ice Cream** recipe for nutrition (page 74)

Slight preparations may be necessary as the activities are adapted to the needs of your classroom.

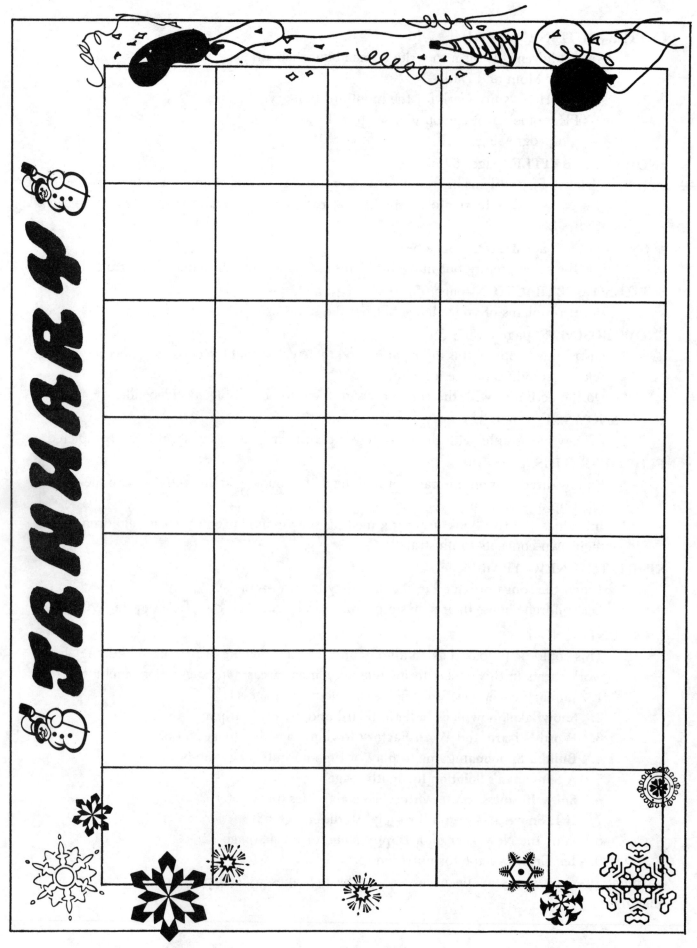

Calendar Creations

JANUARY:

1	New Year's Day
	Emancipation Proclamation signed
	Paul Revere's birthday
	Betsy Ross's birthday
2	Isaac Asimov's birthday
3	Alaska became 49th state
4	First appendectomy performed
	Louis Braille's birthday
5	First woman governor sworn into office (Nellie Ross)
6	Carl Sandburg's birthday
7	Hydrogen bomb developed
9	Richard Nixon's birthday
11	Amelia Earhart became first woman to fly solo across Pacific Ocean
12	First X-ray examination made
14	Henry Ford introduced assembly line
15	Martin Luther King, Jr.'s birthday
16	World Religion Day
17	Benjamin Franklin's birthday
19	Edgar Allen Poe's birthday
20	Sport of basketball invented
22	Lord Byron's birthday
24	Gold discovered in California
29	American League for baseball organized
	First baseball players elected to Baseball Hall of Fame
30	Franklin Delano Roosevelt's birthday

SNEAK PREVIEW OF 19____

(supply date)

YOU WILL NEED:

1. Yellow background
2. Navy blue letters for title
3. White and various shades of blue for large sneaker, contrasting light blue sock with face
4. Several small sneakers and socks (one per child) to display

DIRECTIONS:

Provide each child with a pattern of the sock and sneaker found on the following page. Ask each child to decorate his shoe. Have him write his name on the sock cuff, and write his resolution(s) for the New Year on the lines. Staple the sock to the shoe before it is hung on the bulletin board.

Patterns for
SNEAK
PREVIEW

STUDENT'S NAME

NEW YEAR'S RESOLUTION

SNOWFLAKE

*I'm just a snowflake person
Who fell down from the sky,
With paper, patterns,
    scissors, glue,
You can make me if you try!*

SHOWPLACE

SNOWFLAKE SHOWPLACE

YOU WILL NEED:

1. Dark blue background
2. White letters for title
3. Large white cardboard snowflake person with mittens and stocking cap (could be 3-D if actual clothing was used)
4. Two large packets (for paper and patterns)
5. Several sheets of sturdy white paper for snowflakes and construction paper for patterns found on the following pages

DIRECTIONS:

Ask each child to make a snowflake person by following the directions on pages 49-50. Display finished snowflakes on the bulletin board or around the room. They could also be hung from the ceiling.

Make a Snowflake Person

SNOWFLAKE PERSON
PATTERN

Cut 2 for each child to glue together to make snowperson's body.

SNOWFLAKE PERSON
PATTERN

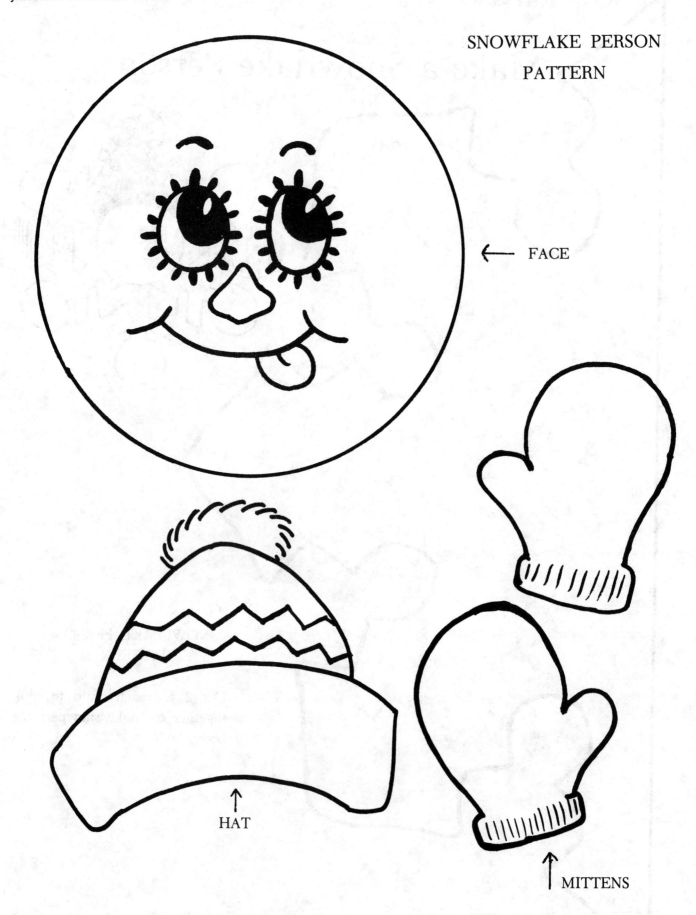

← FACE

HAT

MITTENS

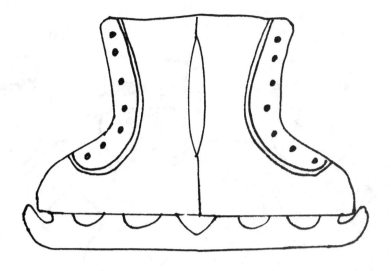

SKATE BORDER

Glide into January with this delightful ice skate border.

To make this bulletin board border, refer to page 9 for directions.

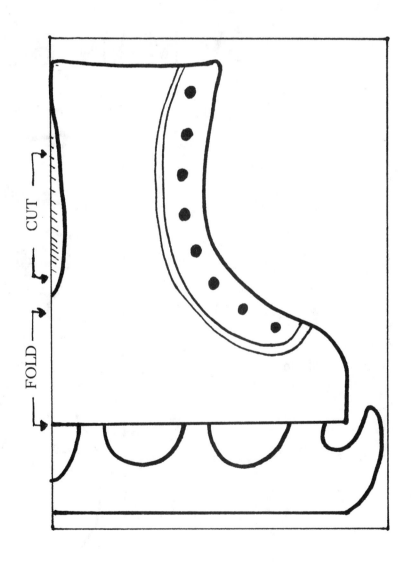

SNOWMAN BORDER

What a cheerful border for a winter bulletin board. Your class will love these cute little snowmen.

To make this border, follow the directions on page 9.

JANUARY

The New Year rolls around once more;
No one knows just what's in store.
Horns and bells ring out at night
As the old year passes out of sight.

Resolutions, big and small,
Are made to last at least till fall.
To listen, to learn, and try our best
To study hard for every test.
To work at home, our folks to please,
Brothers and sisters no more to tease.

At least for January I will try
To live each day as it goes by!

Pur-r-fect Penmanship

53

WORD WIZARD

1. icicle
2. cold
3. January
4. New Year's Day
5. igloo
6. Alaska
7. ice skating
8. Eskimo
9. skiing
10. Louis Braille
11. skis
12. snowmen
13. Carl Sandburg
14. mitten
15. iceberg
16. Richard Nixon
17. polar bear
18. kayak
19. frostbite
20. Dr. Martin Luther King, Jr.
21. penguin
22. mukluks
23. scarf
24. parka
25. Benjamin Franklin
26. ptarmigan
27. albino
28. Robert E. Perry
29. sled
30. Franklin D. Roosevelt

WORD FACTOR

Use the clues to help you find the words to use in the blanks. You will change only one letter each time you solve an answer and move down each list. The final answer in each puzzle will be a winter word.

1.
_ _ _ _ _ _ entire thing
_ _ _ _ _ _ fishlike mammal
_ _ _ _ _ _ layered rock
_ _ _ _ _ _ measures weight
_ _ _ _ _ _ to frighten
_ _ _ _ _ _ cover for neck

2.
_ _ _ _ _ _ past of hear
_ _ _ _ _ _ hidden supply
_ _ _ _ _ _ piece of lumber
_ _ _ _ _ _ wild pigs
_ _ _ _ _ _ ships
_ _ _ _ _ _ rain footwear

3.
_ _ _ _ _ _ mammals that burrow
_ _ _ _ _ _ sticks for flags
_ _ _ _ _ _ lightens in color
_ _ _ _ _ _ steps
_ _ _ _ _ _ knapsacks
_ _ _ _ _ _ recreation areas
_ _ _ _ _ _ Eskimo jacket

4.
_ _ _ _ _ smooth, level
_ _ _ _ _ to fly lightly
_ _ _ _ _ narrow opening
_ _ _ _ _ short act
_ _ _ _ _ footgear for sports

5.
_ _ _ _ _ cloth symbol
_ _ _ _ _ mistake
_ _ _ _ _ cabbage salad
_ _ _ _ _ not fast
_ _ _ _ _ white water vapor

6.
_ _ _ _ skill to draw
_ _ _ _ to perform
_ _ _ _ highest card
_ _ _ _ frozen water

7.
_ _ _ _ _ uncovered
_ _ _ _ _ bundle of hay
_ _ _ _ _ no hair
_ _ _ _ _ brave
_ _ _ _ _ not hot

BUILD A SNOWMAN

Players: 2-4

Directions: Each child playing the game takes a large snowman.

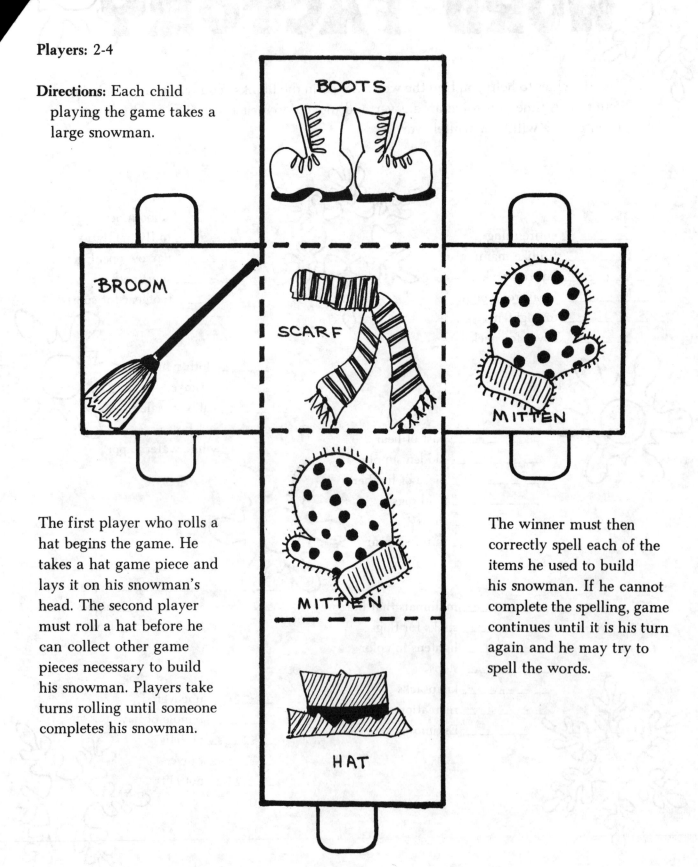

The first player who rolls a hat begins the game. He takes a hat game piece and lays it on his snowman's head. The second player must roll a hat before he can collect other game pieces necessary to build his snowman. Players take turns rolling until someone completes his snowman.

The winner must then correctly spell each of the items he used to build his snowman. If he cannot complete the spelling, game continues until it is his turn again and he may try to spell the words.

Game Piece for "Build a Snowman"

EACH CHILD WILL NEED ONE SNOWMAN! USE OAKTAG FOR PATTERN.

Game Pieces (continued)

You will need to make several of these patterns using oaktag. Color them before they are laminated.

Three CHEERS for the New Year

1. Rah-Rah-Ree,
   Jan-u-ar-y.
   Rah-Rah-Run
   Month number one!

2. W-I-N — T-E-R
   Snow has come again.
   Sledding, skating, snowball fights,
   You can't keep me in!

3. J-A-N-U-A-R-Y
   Starts a New Year passing by.

On the lines below try writing a
cheer of your own. Anything goes...
Your poem does not have to rhyme.
Add motions to your cheer if you like.

_____

_____

_____

_____

_____

_____

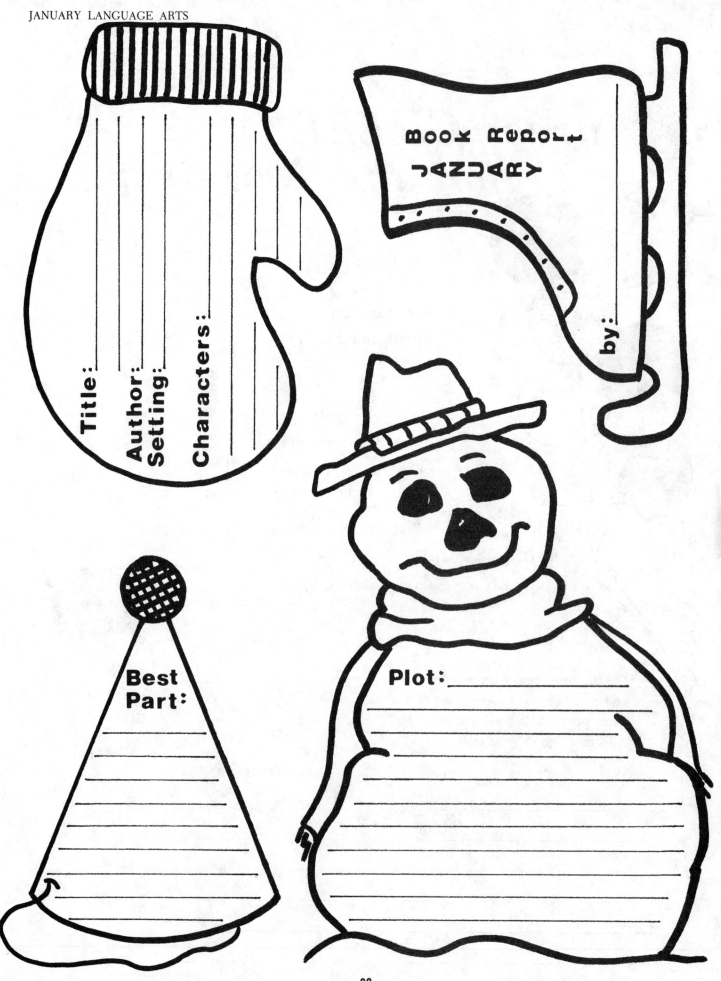

Title:

Author:
Setting:

Characters:

BOOK REPORT
JANUARY

by:

Best
Part:

Plot:

_____
Date

_____ ,

_____

_____

_____

_____

_____

_____

_____

_____

_____ ,

_____

Players: 2-4

Directions:
Roll dice and move that number of spaces. If you land on a space with a star, draw a card and do as it says. If you are correct, stay there. If you are wrong, go back 2 spaces.

FINISH

START

SNOWBALL BATTLE

Sub-zero Subtraction

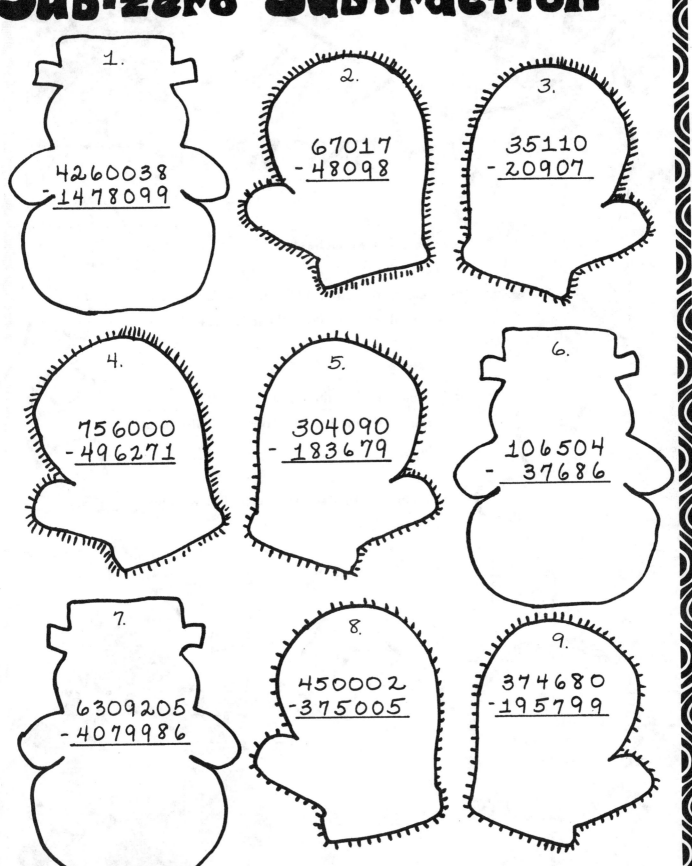

1.
```
  4260038
- 1478099
```

2.
```
  67017
- 48098
```

3.
```
  35110
- 20907
```

4.
```
  756000
- 496271
```

5.
```
  304090
- 183679
```

6.
```
  106504
-  37686
```

7.
```
  6309205
- 4079986
```

8.
```
  450002
- 375005
```

9.
```
  374680
- 195799
```

SNOW ... BUSINESS

SNOW

is water vapor which has frozen forming crystals which have six sides. They look white rather than clear, the color of water, because light shines on all of the sides of the ice crystals and is reflected.

It is amazing that during a storm millions of snowflakes fall and yet every one has a different design.

Cold air makes tiny snowflakes and in warmer weather snowflakes are larger!

Every snowflake is different from every other snowflake!

All snowflakes have six points.

66

SCIENCE in the SNOW

Here are several science activities you might like to try when it snows.

1. Check it out--get a magnifying glass, some dark paper, and some snow. When fresh snow begins to fall, put your dark paper in the freezer for a few minutes until it is cool. Take your dark paper outside and catch a few snowflakes on it. Study them with your magnifying glass.

2. Get two small bowls. In one place an ice cube. In the other put a good-sized snowball. Hold a contest and have students guess which one will melt first and which contained the most water.

3. Bring a little cooking into your classroom. Get some fresh snow and make snow cones (be sure the snow is clean) or try making some ice cream (see directions on page 74).

4. Try this activity indoors or out! Let each student make a snowball. Have a contest to see which student can make his melt the quickest. In a second contest see which child can make his snowball last the longest.

5. Make a snow slide to study under the microscope. Chill a glass slide. When it is cool, catch a snowflake on it. Immediately spray it with hair spray to capture its shape. The snow will melt, but you can study the shape formed by the hair spray under the microscope.

6. Can you guess which colors make snow melt the quickest? Do dark colors absorb moisture and light colors reflect? Try sprinkling several colors of tempera paint in small circles on the snow. Watch for a little while to see what happens. (Dark colors will melt snow first.)

If It Snows...I

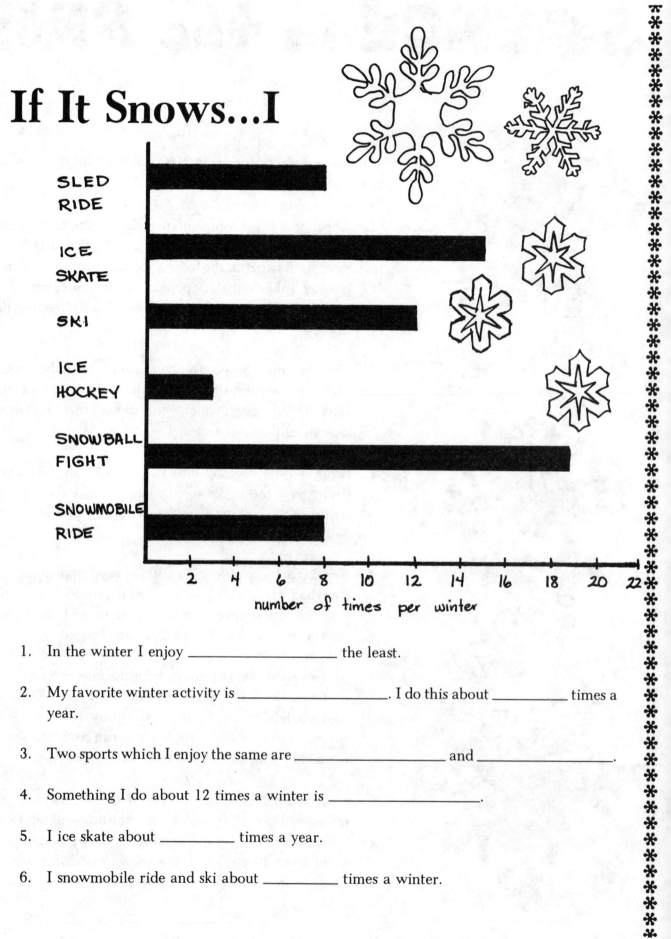

1. In the winter I enjoy _____ the least.

2. My favorite winter activity is _____. I do this about _____ times a year.

3. Two sports which I enjoy the same are _____ and _____.

4. Something I do about 12 times a winter is _____.

5. I ice skate about _____ times a year.

6. I snowmobile ride and ski about _____ times a winter.

A SNOW MOBILE

DIRECTIONS:

1. Cut out 2 snowflakes using this pattern.

2. Fold each snowflake on the dotted line.

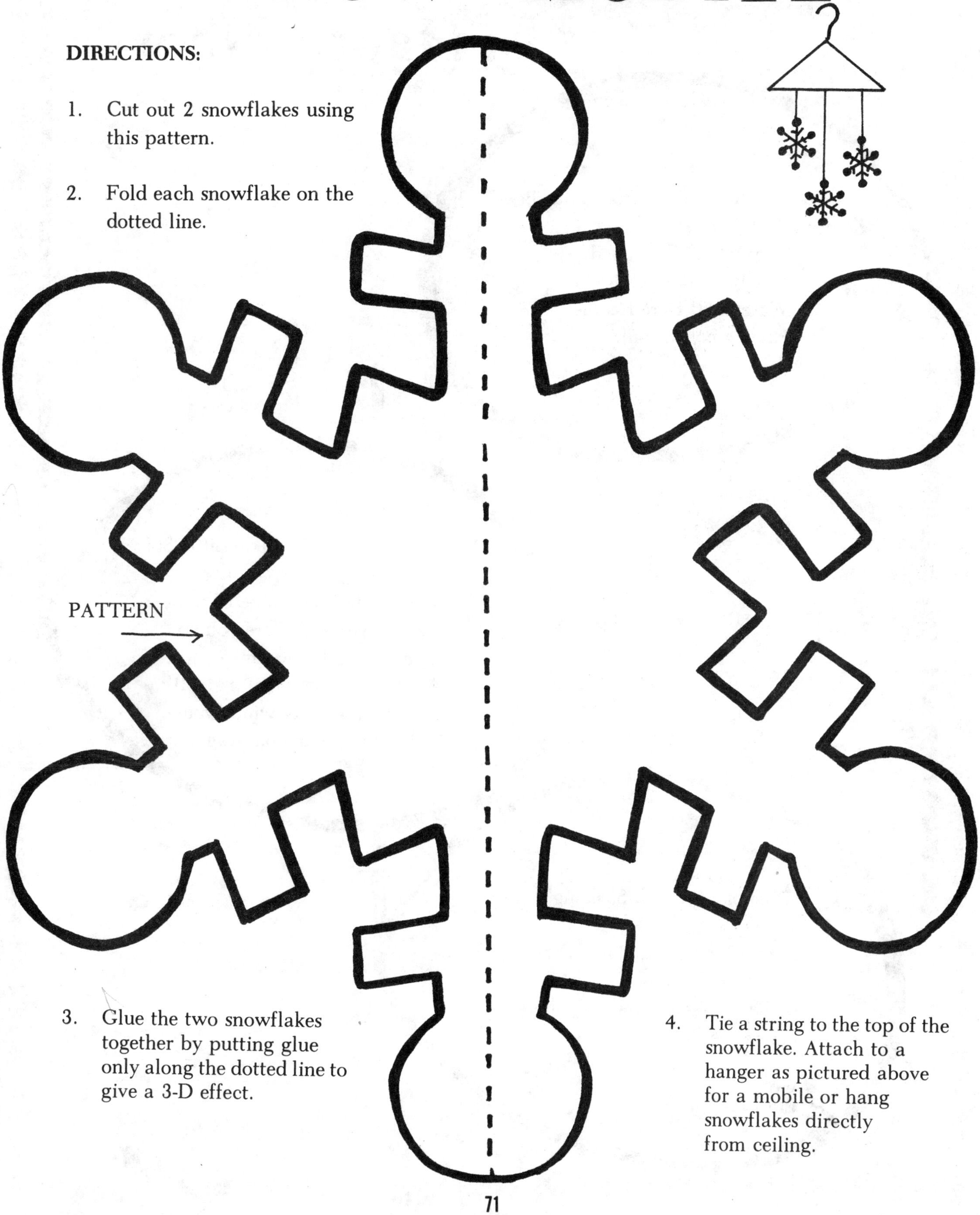

PATTERN →

3. Glue the two snowflakes together by putting glue only along the dotted line to give a 3-D effect.

4. Tie a string to the top of the snowflake. Attach to a hanger as pictured above for a mobile or hang snowflakes directly from ceiling.

Start the New Year on a Happy Note

Tune of "Row, Row, Row Your Boat"

Tug, tug, pull my sled
Slowly up the hill.
Watch out! Here I come!
Hoping not to spill.

Tune of "Twinkle, Twinkle Little Star"

Falling, falling, flakes of snow
How I wonder where you go
Landing on the earth so white,
Melting slowly, what a sight!
Sliding down my windowpane
Winter has come back again.

Tune of "Are You Sleeping"

Happy New Year, Happy New Year
Everyone, Everyone,
January is here, January is here,
Let's have fun! Let's have fun!

WELCOME, MY FRIENDS

Here is a project you'll enjoy making! You'll need a half-gallon milk carton, scissors, a ruler, and some heavy string. After you rinse out the carton, use your ruler to measure a 2½ inch square in one side of the carton. This should be about 1½ inches from the bottom. Cut out the square. Then cut a slit about ¼ inch on each side of the bottom edge. You will form a perch if you bend that edge outward. Follow these same directions to cut out the other three sides.

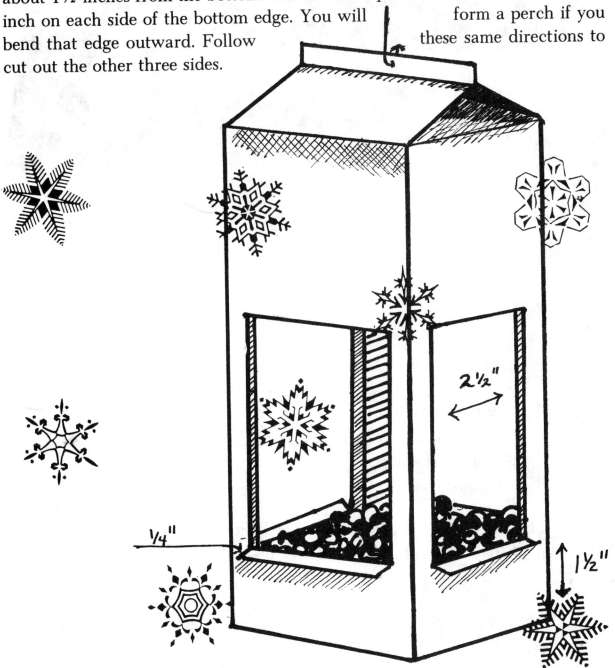

Now you need a small hole punched at the top of the carton. Put a strong cord or heavy string through the hole. Hang feeder in a tree. Fill it with some bird feed. Watch the birds come!

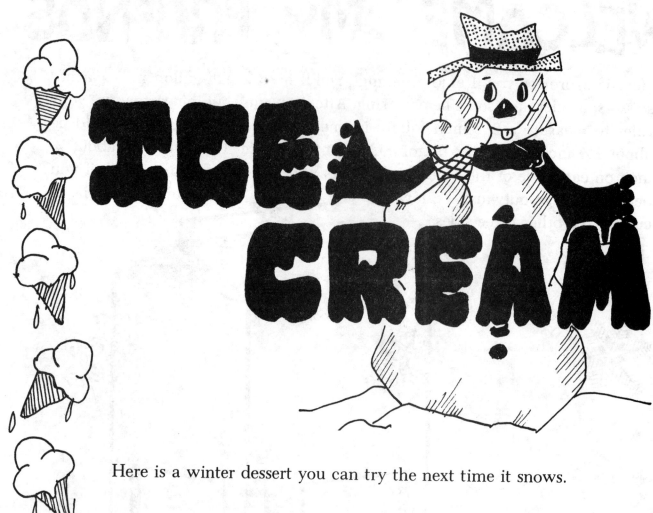

Here is a winter dessert you can try the next time it snows.

Put in a big bowl:

*   4 cups of clean snow
    ½ cup of milk
    2 tablespoons sugar
    1 teaspoon vanilla

Mix the above ingredients, stirring lightly. Eat your treat immediately so it will be fresh. Serve it to 2 or 3 of your friends.

* Be sure that your snow is fresh and not polluted! Check with Mom or Dad.

Suggestions:
1. Use as a ditto for creative writing.
2. Use as a ditto for science experiments about snow/water, evaporation/condensation. Add lines for predictions/outcomes.

Suggestions:
  1. Research penguins and record findings on bird.
  2. Design a winter outfit for a penguin. Use construction paper or material for clothing.

Suggestions:
1. Make learning game for students to match math fact/answer.
2. Use at a language arts center for vocabulary/ definition match game, antonyms, synonyms, homonyms, etc.

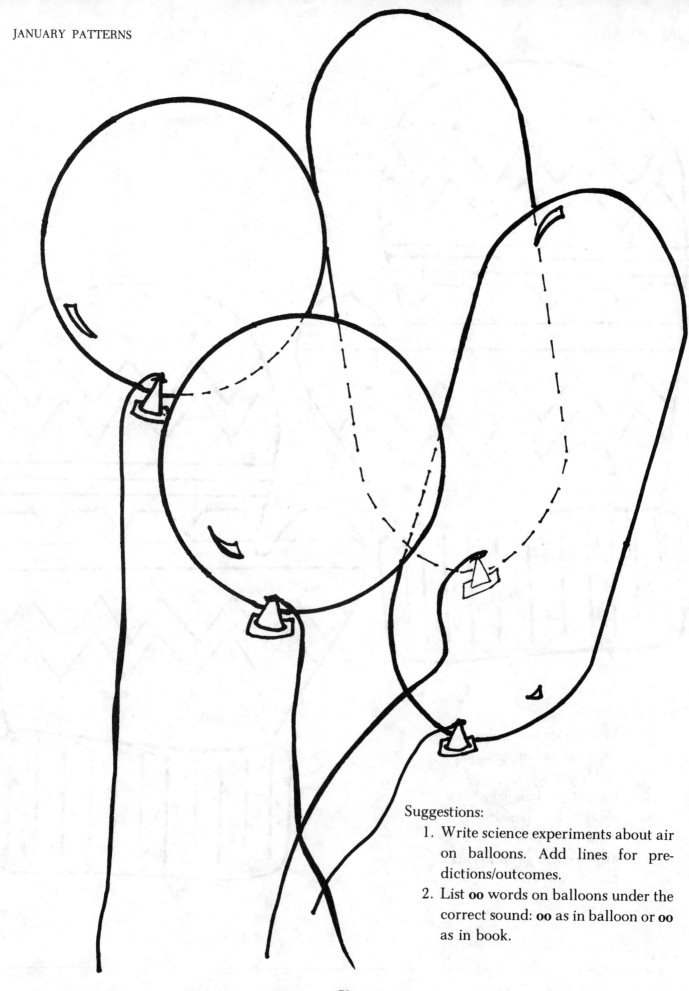

Suggestions:
1. Write science experiments about air on balloons. Add lines for predictions/outcomes.
2. List **oo** words on balloons under the correct sound: **oo** as in balloon or **oo** as in book.

ANSWER KEY

PAGE 55
1. whole
   whale
   shale
   scale
   scare
   scarf

2. heard
   hoard
   board
   boars
   boats
   boots

3. moles
   poles
   pales
   paces
   packs
   parks
   parka

4. flat
   flit
   slit
   skit
   skis

5. flag
   flaw
   slaw
   slow
   snow

6. art
   act
   ace
   ice

7. bare
   bale
   bald
   bold
   cold

PAGE 64
1. 2,538
2. 1,245
3. 1,548
4. 3,468
5. 6,545
6. 2,259
7. 2,238

8. 3,568
9. 2,184
10. 3,663
11. 3,185
12. 5,448

PAGE 65
1. 2,781,939
2. 18,919
3. 14,203
4. 259,729
5. 120,411

6. 68,818
7. 2,229,219
8. 74,997
9. 178,881

PAGE 68
1. ice hockey
2. snowball fighting
   19
3. sled riding
   snowmobile riding
4. ski
5. 15
6. 20

Teacher Tips

FEBRUARY (page 82)
* Use as a coloring sheet.
* Use as a cover for a February booklet of work sheets or projects.

CALENDAR (page 85)
* Add numbers for dates, **Calendar Creations** information (page 86), and/or pictures in appropriate boxes.
* List birthdays of classmates.
* Use as a monthly weather guide.
* Assign research for gifted children to create their own calendar events.

CALENDAR CREATIONS (page 86)
* Allow students to research topics and report findings to class.
* Announce events in opening exercises each day.

WORM WISHES (page 87)
* Make this bulletin board to display names and dates of children celebrating birthdays.

WORM WISHES (card) (page 88)
* Make cards for each child having a birthday this month.
* Let children having birthdays in this month make their own worm wishes cards to display.

HEART STARTERS (page 89)
* Follow directions on the bulletin board sheet to develop this as a creative writing center.
* Change bulletin board title to "Pulsating Problems" and use as a math center.
* Change bulletin board title to "Lovely Work" and display student papers.

I'M HOG WILD ABOUT GOOD WORK (page 90)
* Follow directions on the bulletin board sheets to create this good work area for your students.
* Use this bulletin board with the sheet following "I'm Hog Wild" to display good work in any content area.

PUR-R-FECT PENMANSHIP (page 94)
* Read and discuss the poem orally with your class, discuss format, rhyme, capital letters, and punctuation before assigning children to copy the poem.

WORD WIZARD (page 95)
* Use the words as a spelling list for the month.
* Assign topics for research assignments.
* Use as an answer sheet for **Put Your Heart into It** (page 96).

THE WEATHERMAN (page 97)
* Duplicate this page and **Weatherman Words** (page 98) for a Groundhog Day activity, pasting the correct picture in the appropriate box in the story.

LINCOLN LIMERICKS (page 99)
* Review the limerick pattern after reading limericks to class; assist students with composing their own limericks about Lincoln or perhaps **Word Wizard** ideas.

A "LOVELY" DAY (page 100)
* Duplicate copies for students to read as background information and use in conjunction with **Aiming for Accuracy** sheet (page 101).

LETTER OUTLINE (page 104)
* Give children this form to write home about their progress.

> Dear Mom and Dad,
>
> Here is my work for the month of February.
> Please look at it so you will see how I
> am progressing. . . .

GREAT RACE (page 105)
* Write facts about Washington and Lincoln on cards and use the gameboard as a social studies review.
* Write a number in each space and have students add, multiply, or complete various operations as they move from the President to the heart.
* Give each student a blank gameboard and allow him time to establish game rules, game pieces, and concepts to be learned, such as spelling words, math facts, etc.

PICTURE PERFECT (page 106)
* Use the same picture but make problems easier or more difficult to suit grade level.

PROBLEMS OF PRESIDENTS (page 107)
* Write a word problem in each space for children to solve.
* In each blank write a problem Washington or Lincoln faced for children to research and find an appropriate solution.

HIBERNATION (page 108)
* Use on February 2 to supplement **The Weatherman** language arts activity.

THE HEART (page 109)
* Give each child a copy of this information to study before he completes **Open Heart Surgery** activity (pages 110-111).

OPEN HEART SURGERY (pages 110-111)
* Reproduce both heart drawings for each child; explain that these papers are to be glued together around the edges only. Have each student number a sheet of paper to six; then identify each part of the heart labeled. This activity could be used as a test! Cut open the heart and check answers.

FEBRUARY PRESIDENTS (page 112)
* Review with students the skill of reading a table or chart before assigning this work sheet.

HAPPY HEART (page 118)
* Duplicate this page for students at the beginning of February to encourage good citizenship as they cut apart the tasks and follow the directions given.

MINI UNIT--THE HEART
This could be prepared as an all-day unit for intermediate or primary children. Choose work sheets in this packet to include all content areas. Our suggestions include:
1. **February** cover sheet for booklet about the heart (page 82)
2. **Heart Starters** bulletin board and creative writing ideas (page 89)
3. **Word Wizard** and **Put Your Heart into It** crossword puzzle (pages 95, 96)
4. A **"Lovely" Day** and **Aiming for Accuracy** for language arts (pages 100, 101)
5. **Heart Attracts** for language arts (page 102)
6. **Picture Perfect** for math (page 106)
7. **The Heart** and **Open Heart Surgery for Science** (pages 109, 110-111)
8. **A Valentine Necklace** art project (page 115)
9. **Love Songs** work sheet for music (page 116)

Slight preparations may be necessary as the activities are adapted to your classroom.

Calendar Creations ♥♥♥

FEBRUARY:	1	Langston Hughes' birthday
	2	Groundhog Day
	4	Charles Lindbergh's birthday
	6	National Association for Advancement of Colored People formed
	7	Laura Ingalls Wilder's birthday
		Charles Dickens' birthday
		George Herman (Babe) Ruth's birthday
	8	Boy Scouts of America founded
	9	U. S. Weather Service established
	10	First fire extinguisher patented by Virginia Crane
	11	Thomas Edison's birthday
		First U. S. hospital opened (Pennsylvania Hospital)
	12	Abraham Lincoln's birthday
	14	Valentine's Day
	15	Susan B. Anthony's birthday
	16	Patent for nylon given to Wallace Carothers
	17	Stethoscope invented by René Laënnec
	18	Pluto discovered by Clyde Tombaugh
		Chinese New Year begins
	20	U. S. Post Office established
	21	Washington Monument dedicated
		Malcolm X assassinated
	22	George Washington's birthday
		Popcorn (popped corn) introduced by Indians
		First five-and-ten-cent store opened (Woolworth)
	25	Pierre Renoir's birthday
	26	"Buffalo Bill" William Cody's birthday
		Grand Canyon National Park established in Arizona
	27	John Steinbeck's birthday
	28	Mario Andretti's birthday
	29	Extra day due to Leap Year

Special Events:	Black History Month
	American Music Month
	Brotherhood Week
	Dental Health Week

WORM WISHES FOR YOUR BIRTHDAY

YOU WILL NEED:

1. Brown letters for title
2. Light blue background
3. Brown worm holding small red or pink hearts
4. Several small worms to display names of students having birthdays this month

DIRECTIONS:

Display worms with names and dates of children celebrating birthdays.
Give each child a card to complete. (Pattern next page.)

"Worm Wishes on Your Birthday!"

HEART STARTERS

YOU WILL NEED:

1. Red letters for title
2. Pink background
3. Red and black heart, legs, arms, accessories
4. Several small red hearts on which to display story starters

DIRECTIONS:

Write these story starters on the small red hearts to display as creative writing topics: When I took a trip inside the heart I saw...; The heart can be called a pump because...; Cupid's recipe for love is...; I just love to...; One Valentine's Day I met a cupid who...; I would love to buy a box of candy for...; As I was walking down the street one day I saw a heart that was...

I'M HOG WILD ABOUT GOOD WORK

YOU WILL NEED:

1. Brown letters for title
2. Turquoise blue background
3. Large brown ground hog with shadow
4. Yellow sun
5. Several copies of the following page on which good work is done to display on bulletin board

DIRECTIONS:

Give each child a copy of the following page on which he completes a particular assignment. You may wish to add lines for creative writing, small suns which contain math problems, etc. Adapt the sheet to suit the individual needs of your class.

HEART BORDER

A lovely scene will be these lacey little hearts on your valentine bulletin board.

For directions to make this attractive border, refer to page 9.

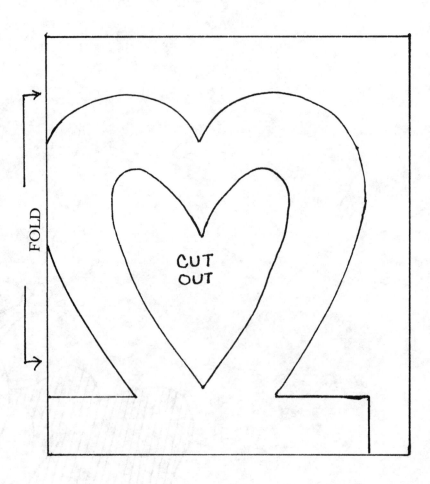

FOLD

CUT OUT

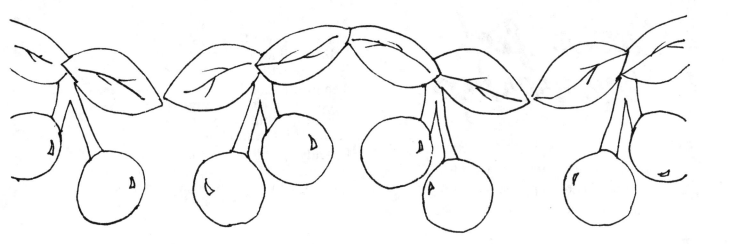

CHERRY BORDER

All attention will focus on this eye-catching holiday border.

Refer to page 9 for directions to complete such a "cheer"y border.

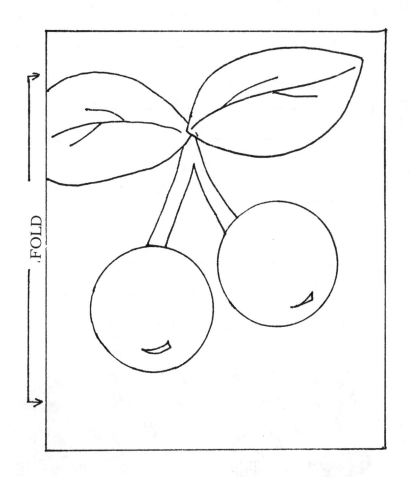

Pwr-r-fect Penmanship

Read the poem several times to yourself. Then copy the poem on the lines below.

FEBRUARY

Around the yard drifts mounting snow,
The chilly wind does softly blow,
February has come once more
Bringing with it Lincoln lore.

The groundhog from his burrow creeps
Up to the surface he shyly peeps,
The sun is shining overhead.
Hello, Winter. Back to bed!

Friendships bloom, romances start,
Around the room are cupids and hearts
Made for loved ones far and near —
Valentine's Day is almost here.

WORD WIZARD

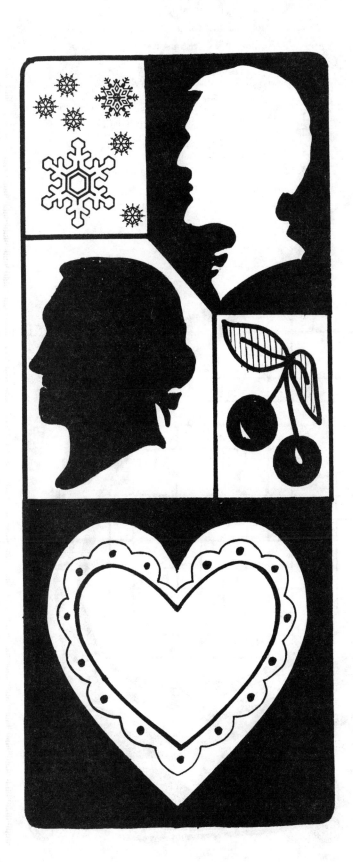

1. Groundhog Day
2. February
3. Valentine's Day
4. George Washington
5. Abraham Lincoln
6. shadow
7. Susan B. Anthony
8. cupid
9. hibernate
10. stethoscope
11. sweetheart
12. post office
13. leap year
14. burrow
15. monument
16. Malcolm X
17. president
18. Charles Lindbergh
19. brotherhood
20. Thomas Edison
21. Charles Dickens
22. Boy Scouts
23. Renoir
24. winter
25. cherry tree
26. Laura Ingalls Wilder
27. Galileo
28. heart
29. Helen Keller
30. John Glenn

PUT YOUR HEART INTO IT...

ACROSS:

3. Building for mail
6. National Association for Advancement of Colored People
7. Popular animal on February 2
8. John _____ - 1st American to orbit the earth
12. Shade of an object
13. 16th U.S. President
16. To spend the winter sleeping
17. Instrument used to hear heartbeat
19. French painter
20. Coldest season of year
21. Second month (abbreviation)
23. _____ B. Anthony
24. Kind of tree Washington cut

DOWN:

1. First U.S. President
2. Another name for groundhog
4. Author of **A Christmas Carol**
5. Abbreviation for President
9. Greeting card sent February 14
10. _____ Steinbeck, author
11. Popped corn
14. _____ Abe, nickname
15. Helen _____ (deaf and blind)
18. Laura Ingalls _____, author of children's books
22. Boy Scouts of America (abbreviation)

THE WEATHERMAN

[1] day Mr. [2] woke up from his nap. He had been [3] for a long time. He lived in a [4] in the [5]. He looked out of his [6]. The [7] was so bright that he saw his [8]. Mr. [9] went to [10] for [11] more weeks of [12].

WEATHERMAN WORDS

ground   one   sleeping

winter   hole   groundhog

burrow   bed   shadow

groundhog   sun   six

98

LINCOLN LIMERICKS

The LIMERICK is a five-line poem with a rhyme pattern A-A-B-B-A. Clap your hands as you read each line and write the number of syllables you hear in each line on the blank.

There once was a man, Abe Lincoln ____
Who had a habit of thinkin' ____
'That one day he'd be ____
Someone famous, you see, ____
And now he's called President Lincoln. ____

There once was a Great Emancipator ____
Who was also a superb debater ____
The slaves he set free ____
In our own great country ____
The 16th President -- none greater! ____

Now try to write your own limerick in the space below. Be sure to check your rhyme pattern and the number of syllables.

_____

_____

_____

_____

_____

99

A "LOVELY" DAY

BE MY VALENTINE. This expression can be heard often on February 14. Greeting cards sent to friends or sweethearts are called valentines. Many of these cards are very decorative with tender verses, while others are humorous cards with a less serious message.

Although many countries celebrate this holiday, customs vary. In the U.S. and Canada, children design valentine boxes and cards, send candy, and sometimes enjoy a party or a dance. In England children exchange gifts such as candy or fruit. Young maidens in Italy awaken early to watch from their windows for a man to pass, hoping that he will marry her during the next year. Finally in Denmark a kind of valentine known as a **gaekkebrev** (joke letter) is sent unsigned to a friend. Other Danes mail snowdrop flowers which have been pressed. Most Valentine's Day customs are associated with love or the hopes of finding romance.

Romans celebrated February 15 in a festival called **Lupercalia** which honored Juno, goddess of women and marriage, and the god of nature, Pan. This was a lover's festival for young people. Later the celebration was changed to February 14, St. Valentine's Day. The pagan ideas, though, still remain today.

Early study shows there were two St. Valentines. The first St. Valentine was a priest who lived in Rome during the 200's. He was imprisoned for helping Christians. Legend states that he cured the jailkeeper's daughter of her blindness. He was later beheaded. The second St. Valentine was a bishop near Rome. He was killed for spreading Christianity to Roman families.

Aiming for Accuracy

1. A valentine is a
   a) greeting card   b) fable   c) fire

2. The goddess of women and marriage is
   a) Cupid   b) Pan   c) Juno

3. People who believe in Christ are
   a) Lupercalians   b) pagans   c) Christians

4. Valentine's Day is usually celebrated
   a) January 25   b) February 14   c) twice a year

5. Historians think St. Valentine
   a) was a Roman clergyman   b) never lived
   c) lives today

6. A person who worships many gods is
   a) pagan   b) Christian   c) Danish

DRAW CUSTOMS

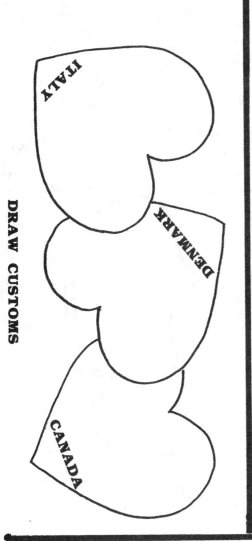

ITALY

DENMARK

CANADA

VALENTINE VOCABULARY

1.	VALENTINE	a. joke letter
2.	TENDER	b. healed
3.	HUMOROUS	c. greeting card
4.	VARY	d. connected with
5.	MAIDEN	e. jailed
6.	GAEKKEBREV	f. unmarried girl
7.	IMPRISONED	g. funny
8.	BEHEADED	h. had the head removed
9.	ASSOCIATED	i. loving
10.	CURED	j. change

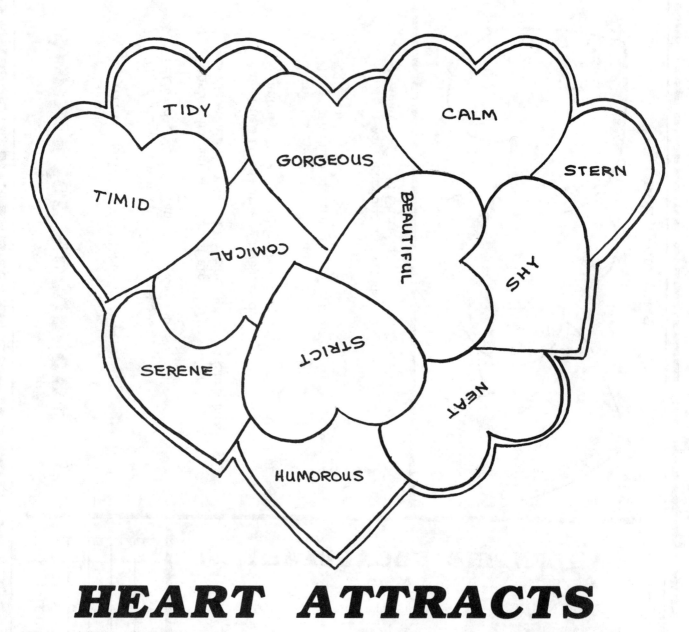

HEART ATTRACTS

Write each pair of synonyms on the line. Then write one antonym in the blank at the end.

1. _____ _____

2. _____ _____

3. _____ _____

4. _____ _____

5. _____ _____

6. _____ _____

Title: _____
Author: _____
Setting: _____

Characters: _____

_____
_____
_____

Best Part: |||||||||

Plot: _____
_____
_____
_____
_____
_____
_____
_____
_____
_____
_____
_____
_____

February Book Report

by: _____
_____

Date

_____ ,

_____ ,

START

GREAT
RACE

START

105

PICTURE PERFECT

NAME

DATE

Solve each problem. Then shade in the
answers below to find the hidden picture.

1. 368
   -179

2. 587
   -368

3. 523
   -237

4. 328
   -297

5. 693
   -584

6. 755
   -326

7. 902
   -357

8. 767
   -493

9. 763
   -295

10. 731
    -286

11. 935
    -547

12. 832
    -649

13. 583
    -127

14. 984
    -796

15. 805
    -367

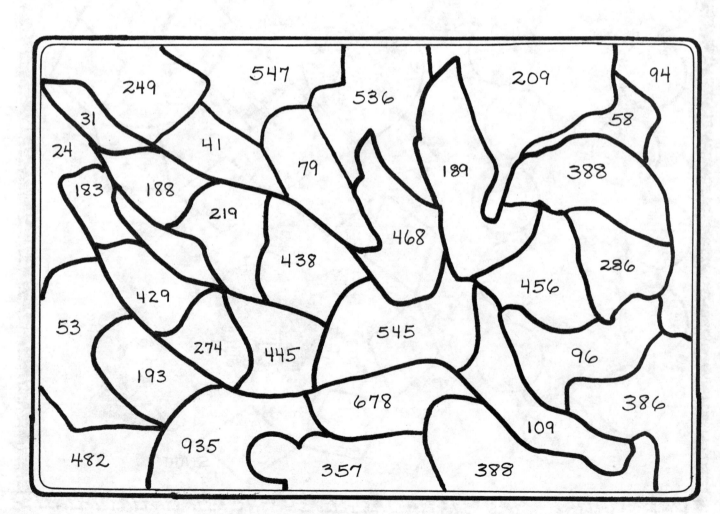

_____

NAME

_____

DATE

Problems
of
Presidents

HIBERNATION

Many animals sleep or go into a "trance" during the long cold months. This winter sleep is called **HIBERNATION**. The groundhog is one of the best hibernators.

   * Choose one of the hibernating animals listed below. Study it. Then write 5 facts you learned about it.

   * Put an X on the animal below that doesn't hibernate in the winter.

1. _____

2. _____

3. _____

4. _____

5. _____

THE
HEART

The main organ of the circulatory system is the heart. The heart acts like a pump. With each beat blood is pushed through the blood vessels into every part of the body.

The heart is divided into four main parts, or chambers. Each of the two parts at the top is called the **ATRIUM**. Blood flows into each atrium from the blood vessels. The two parts at the bottom of the heart are known as the **VENTRICLES**.

The heart has two parts that behave like doors that open only one way. These are **VENTRICLES**. They keep blood moving in the correct direction. The **AORTA** is the main artery of the body. It carries blood from the left ventricle to all organs except the lungs.

Study the following heart diagrams and this information sheet. Then complete the OPEN HEART SURGERY lesson.

Your heart is the size of a fist.

Your heart beats about 70 times a minute.

Your heart beats approximately 100,000 times a day!

Open Heart Surgery

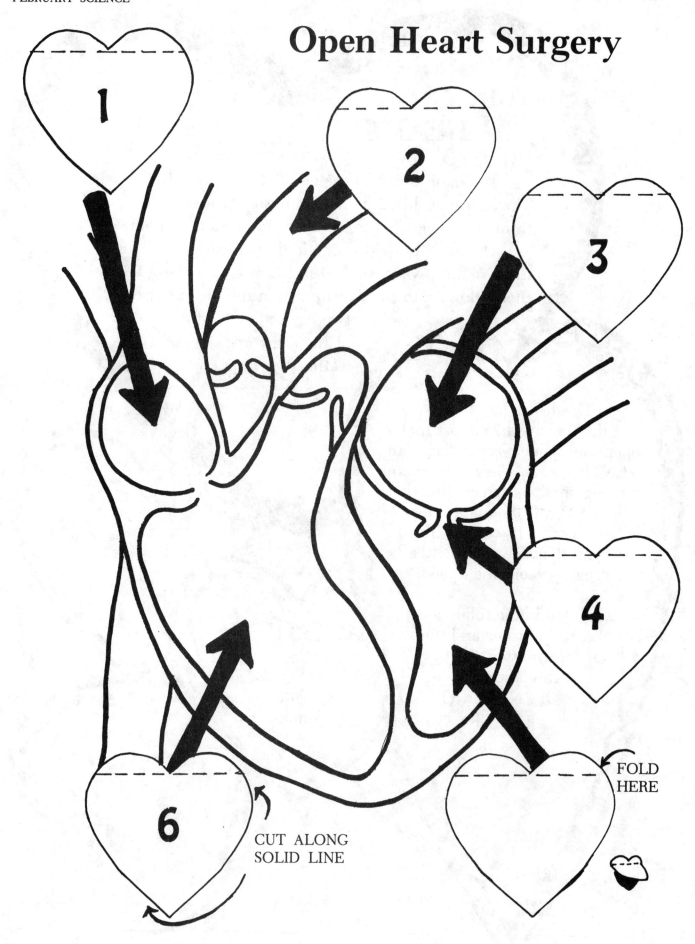

1

2

3

4

6

FOLD
HERE

CUT ALONG
SOLID LINE

Open Heart Surgery

RIGHT
ATRIUM

AORTA

LEFT
ATRIUM

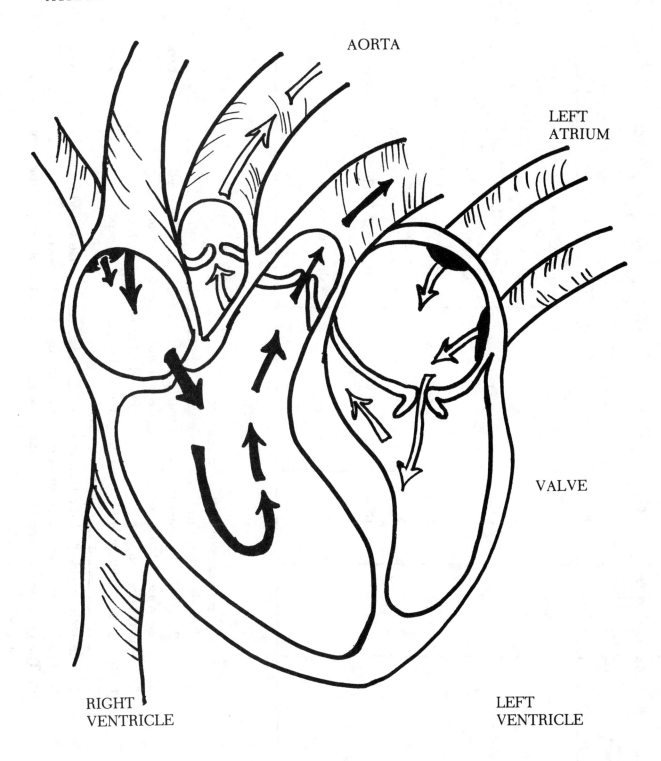

VALVE

RIGHT
VENTRICLE

LEFT
VENTRICLE

FEBRUARY PRESIDENTS

NAME	BORN	DIED	BIRTHPLACE	MAJOR ACCOMPLISHMENTS
LINCOLN, Abraham	1809	1865	Kentucky	Gettysburg Address, Freed slaves, Established first military draft, 16th President (1861-1865)
WASHINGTON, George	1732	1799	Virginia	Commander in Chief of first American Army, 1st President (1789-1797), Organized first census
KENNEDY, John F.	1917	1963	Massachusetts	Youngest elected President, 35th President (1961-1963), Cuban Missile Crisis, Nixon-Kennedy Debates
JEFFERSON, Thomas	1743	1826	Virginia	Author of Declaration of Independence, Architect of Monticello, Established West Point, 3rd President (1801-1809)

1. Which President served the shortest term? _____
2. Two Presidents born in Virginia were _____ and _____.
3. The President who lived the longest was _____. He lived _____ years.
4. George Washington died _____ years before Lincoln was born.
5. Thomas Jefferson was the _____ President of the United States.
6. All the Presidents named above served a total of _____ years.
7. _____ lived to be 67 years old.
8. The 16th President of the U.S. was _____. He served for _____ years.
9. The President born in the most northern state listed above was _____.
10. The difference in age between the President who was the oldest and the President who was the youngest is _____ years.

112

VALENTINE BASKET

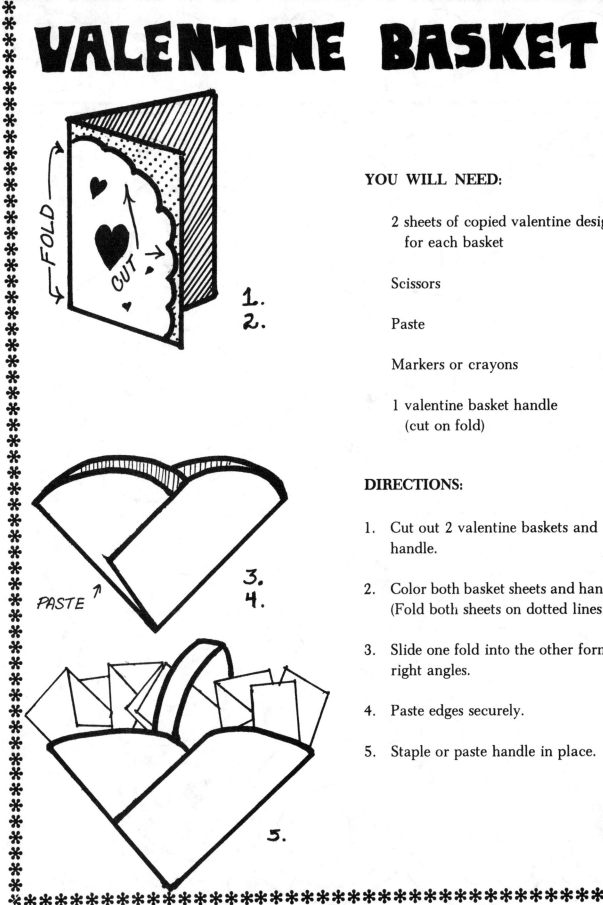

1.
2.

YOU WILL NEED:

2 sheets of copied valentine design
for each basket

Scissors

Paste

Markers or crayons

1 valentine basket handle
(cut on fold)

DIRECTIONS:

1. Cut out 2 valentine baskets and
handle.

2. Color both basket sheets and handles.
(Fold both sheets on dotted lines.)

3. Slide one fold into the other forming
right angles.

4. Paste edges securely.

5. Staple or paste handle in place.

PASTE

3.
4.

5.

BASKET
HANDLE
(place on fold)

VALENTINE BASKET
pattern

A Valentine Neckline

YOU WILL NEED:

Yarn (red or white)
Needle with big eye
Toothpicks
Waxed paper
Dough (recipe follows)
Cookie Sheet

DOUGH RECIPE

Mix: ⅔ cup salt
         ½ cup flour
         ⅓ cup water
         several drops of red food
             coloring

NOTE: This dough recipe can be
         prepared in advance and
         stored for a few days in a
         plastic bag in the
         refrigerator. Let stand at
         room temperature the day
         of use.

DIRECTIONS:

1. Take a small amount of dough and mold it into the shape of a heart (or other valentine design).
2. Gently puncture the heart, before it dries, with a toothpick.
3. Bake designs for one hour at 350°.
4. Use acrylics and paint designs. Let dry.
5. Thread with yarn before wearing.

LOVE SONGS

NAME A SONG WITH "LOVE" IN THE TITLE.

1. _____
2. _____

3. _____
4. _____

5. _____
6. _____

7. _____
8. _____

NAME A SONG WITH "HEART" IN THE TITLE.

1. _____
2. _____

3. _____
4. _____

5. _____
6. _____

7. _____
8. _____

116

A VALENTINE SONG

Sing this song to the tune of "It's a Small World." You may wish to add piano or guitar accompaniment.

1 It's a day of laughter,
  A day of fun.
  It's a day for love
  Shared with everyone.
  Though it comes once a year
  Valentine's Day brings cheer.
  It's a fun, fun day.

Chorus:
  It's a fun day, yes, indeed,
  It's a fun day, yes, indeed,
  It's a fun day, yes, indeed,
  It's a fun, fun day.

2 There are silly little cards
  And some serious ones, too,
  That we carefully choose
  For friends old and new.
  And there are presents, flowers, candy
  For those folks we think are dandy;
  It's a fun, fun day.

Chorus:

HAPPY HEART

Give someone in the class a compliment.

Do something special for your teacher.

Make a valentine and give it to your mom.

Tutor a classmate who needs help.

Complete an assignment today for extra credit.

Call your grandparents and wish them a happy day.

Do something special for your pet today.

Visit a neighbor today.

Read a story to a younger brother, sister, or student.

Share part of your lunch or snack with a friend.

Feed the birds! They need love, too!

Write a poem or love note to someone.

DIRECTIONS:

Cut out the heart with all of the notes attached. Each day cut off one of the strips and follow the directions on it.

Suggestions:
1. Use as a background for a valentine card.
2. Use as a pattern to make large heart from oaktag. Attach smaller hearts to form mobile.

FOLD

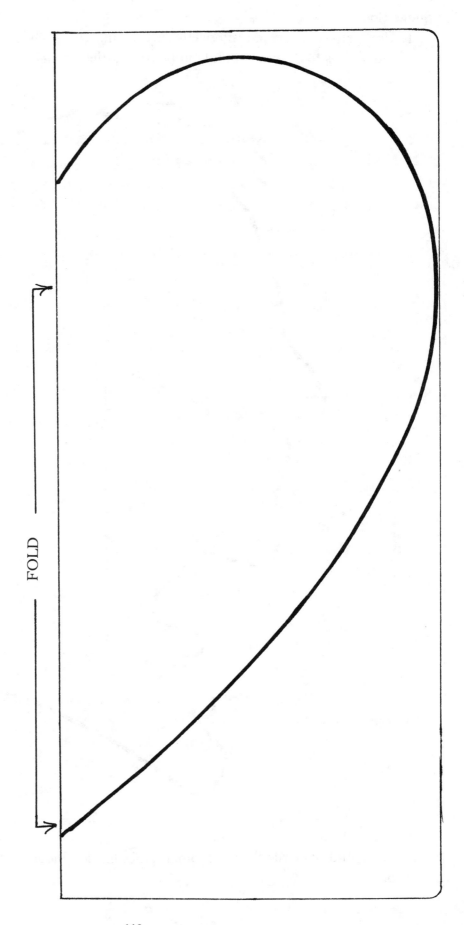

119

Suggestions:

1. Use pattern to teach silhouette art form. Have children make silhouettes of themselves to display on bulletin board entitled "Celebrity Silhouettes."

2. Have students write their autobiographies inside silhouettes they made in suggestion one.

Suggestions:

1. Use pattern to teach silhouette art form. Make silhouettes of other famous people for children to identify and/or research. Place silhouettes on bulletin board or at a learning center.

2. Place silhouettes of Washington and Lincoln on bulletin board. Cut apart strips stating facts of these Presidents. Children must correctly place strip under President it describes. Answers should be written on backs of strips for self-check.

Suggestions:
  1. Use oaktag patterns with large heart to construct mobiles to hang in room.

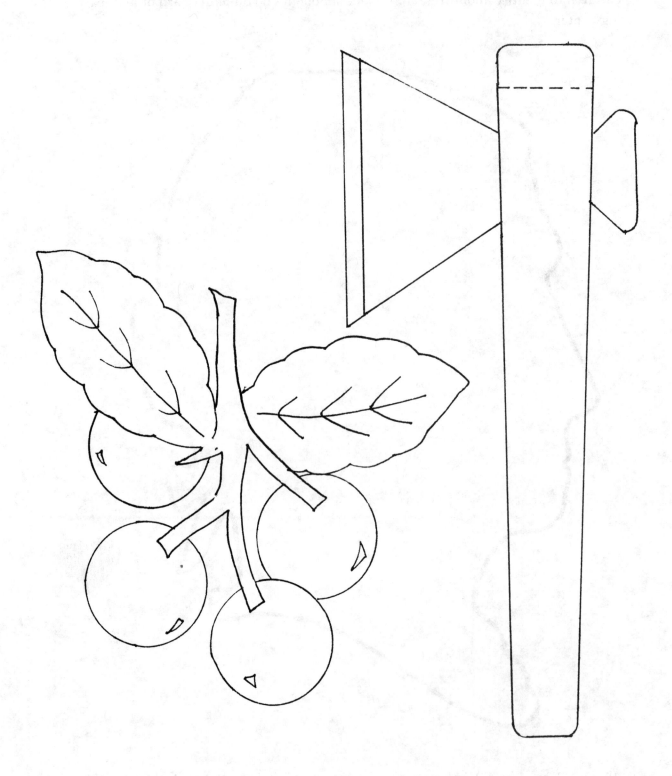

  2. Write forms of discipline on patterns. Use the hatchet to list small tasks for improper behavior, and write various types of rewards on cherries for good behavior.

Suggestions:
  1. Use in conjunction with a lesson about letter writing: addressing envelopes.
  2. Use as a bulletin board for pen pals. Place large mailbox on board and on envelope pattern place names and addresses of pen pals. Add letters from pen pals to bulletin board as they are received.

ANSWER KEY

PAGE 96

ACROSS
3. post office
6. N.A.A.C.P
7. groundhog
8. Glenn
12. shadow
13. Lincoln
16. hibernate
17. stethoscope
19. Renoir
20. winter
21. Feb.
23. Susan
24. cherry

DOWN
1. Washington
2. woodchuck
4. Charles Dickens
5. Pres.
9. valentine
10. John
11. popcorn
14. honest
15. Keller
18. Wilder
22. B.S.A.

PAGE 97
1. One
2. groundhog
3. sleeping
4. burrow
5. ground
6. hole

7. sun
8. shadow
9. groundhog
10. bed
11. six
12. winter

PAGE 101
1. a
2. c
3. c
4. b
5. a
6. a

1. c
2. i
3. g
4. j
5. f
6. a
7. e
8. h
9. d
10. b

PAGE 102
1. tidy-neat
2. gorgeous-beautiful
3. calm-serene
4. stern-strict
5. timid-shy
6. comical-humorous
Antonyms will vary.

PAGE 106
1. 189
2. 219
3. 286
4. 31
5. 109
6. 429
7. 545
8. 274

9. 468
10. 445
11. 388
12. 183
13. 456
14. 188
15. 438

PAGE 108
Raccoon does not hibernate.

PAGE 110-111
Self-checking when hearts are opened.

PAGE 112
1. Kennedy
2. Washington
   Jefferson
3. Jefferson
   83
4. 10
5. 3rd

6. 22
7. Washington
8. Lincoln
   4
9. Kennedy
10. 37